10 9 8 7 6 5 4 3 2 1

Copyright© 2024 by CHEETAH® Toys & More, LLC.

ISBN-13: 978-1-964243-70-2
ISBN 10: 1-964243-70-2

Permission request(s) should be submitted to the publisher in writing at one of the addresses below:

CHEETAH® Toys & More, LLC
c/o Upper Albany Merchants Association
1382 Albany Ave, 2nd floor
Hartford, CT 06112

Port Antonio PO
Portland, Jamaica

info@mycheetahinc.com
paulettetrowers@yahoo.com
WhatsApp: 860-781-1726 / 876-909-6311

Authors: Paulette Trowers, Juris Doctor; Kristina Jaz; Iain Taylor
Editor: Fiona Porter-Lawson
Reviewers: Nicheisha Miller-Griffiths, Dr. Carol Clarke, Yanique Wallace, Janice Trowers, Ed.s, M.Ed
Book Designer: Feri Setiawan
Chief Illustrator: Tooba Zaib
Cover and interior design: CHEETAH® Purrrrrrr Publishing ("CHEETAH®"), an imprint of CHEETAH® Toys & More, LLC.
Publisher: CHEETAH® (Connect to Higher Education, Electronic Tools, Application & Help)

This book belongs to:

Name:

....

School:

....

Date:

....

Table of Contents

Table of Contents

Education is the key that opens doors no child should ever find locked.
Paulette Trowers

Dear CHEETAH® family,

CHEETAH® Toys & More, LLC ("CHEETAH®") is proud to introduce JamDER+ (Jamaican Decodable & Early Readers), an innovative programme that aligns with the Ministry of Education, Skills, Youth & Information's (MoESYI) new literacy initiative. CHEETAH® produces educational content under its imprint, CHEETAH® Purrrrrrr Publishing. FastTrack Literacy is the company's umbrella reading programme, while JamDER+ is the customised version for Jamaica.

CHEETAH® builds on decades of proven strategies and integrates MoESYI's "Clusters for Teaching Phonemes" to deliver a pupil-centred approach to teaching and learning. It is grounded in international best practice and the science of reading.

Over two decades ago, a National Reading Panel (NRP) in the USA published a report detailing its evidence-based assessment of the scientific literature and its implications for reading instruction. We often see this study's findings as an infographic titled "The Five Pillars of Early Literacy". These five pillars — phonemic awareness, phonics, fluency, vocabulary and comprehension — are central to JamDER+'s design and delivery.

https://www.reallygreatreading.com/content/what-are-five-pillars-reading

Adaptive Technology: A World-First in Literacy

In addition to our physical and eBooks, CHEETAH® has created two new GPTs (Generative Pre-trained Transformers), a world-first in literacy education, as described below. The prompts will be given to our partners. These are adapted specifically for literacy and are customised and globally unique; the first of their kind anywhere in the world.

- **FastTrack Literacy P1–P2 Flow©** – A teacher-focused tool with built-in automated prompts to help educators generate new, age-appropriate diagnostic passages.

- **CHEETAH® Reading Partner©** – A pupil-centred companion that not only creates an initial diagnostic story for each letter, but also provides comprehension checks, personalised reading plans, log sheets, motivational feedback, and opportunities for pupils to author their own stories. Together, these GPTs blend decades of evidence-based literacy with adaptive AI technology, offering educators and parents tested prompts with programmed steps, while giving pupils a highly personalised path to fluency.

✓ **Phonemic Awareness:** Pupils learn how to produce each sound. They listen for instances of the sound during teacher read-alouds, and then determine where in the word the sound is located (beginning, middle, end). Pupils get unlimited practice with GPT integrated.

✓ **Phoneme Segmentation:** This includes conducting a pupil activity to identify sounds within words and practising segmenting and blending sounds. We recommend that teachers start the year modeling the use of the tool below until pupils can complete a given word set independently. The tools below can also be used as formative assessments.

Word	Letters				Number of sounds
bump	b	u	m	p	4
chill	ch	i	ll		3
duck	d	u	ck		3
happy	h	a	pp	y	4
cat	c	a	t		3

Say & tap · Map (sounds) · Graph (letters) · Check · Write it

Say It & Tap It					
Map It					
Graph It					
Check It	Sound			Letter	
Write It					

With the integration of GPT, CHEETAH® will explain how to integrate technology to give pupils multiple chances to practise.

✓ Fluency: The rate (how fast) at which pupils read, their accuracy (saying the correct word), and prosody (intonation, expression, phrasing) are all components of fluent reading. Within JamDER+, there are several opportunities to monitor and strengthen fluency:

- Diagnostic story – An age-appropriate diagnostic story is presented at the beginning of the book to assess prior learning and guide personalised lessons.
- Phoneme passages – For each letter phoneme, pupils read a short passage that uses simple CVC and sight words at Level 1. Each passage is accompanied by a Teacher Focus Box outlining the word count, key words, tricky words, and the Flesch Reading Ease score.
- Progress fluency test – At the end of each set of sounds from Set 2 onwards, another fluency test is included to measure progress.
- Digital support – Pupils have access to the iCHEETAH© device and the proprietary ChatGPT prompt. The FastTrack Literacy GPT (AI learning assistant) and accompanying mobile app are pending release.

✓ Vocabulary: Pupils encounter new words in each thematic unit, in our books and online, and may be assessed formally or informally using the suggested vocabulary from both the Teacher's and Pupil's Helper. This systematic approach builds essential background knowledge, enabling pupils to comprehend texts more effectively.

✓ Comprehension: In every sound set, pupils practise oral and written comprehension questions by following teacher instructions, working with partners, sharing ideas in groups and using CHEETAH® Reading Partner©. JamDER+ reinforces comprehension through targeted questions included in our decodable stories and readers. During the early stages of literacy, comprehension is taught alongside but distinctly from phonemic awareness and phonics, ensuring that pupils not only decode words but also understand what they read. They are guided to make meaning from text through discussion, visualization, and connection to real-life experiences, laying the foundation for critical thinking and deeper understanding. These intentional opportunities allow pupils to engage in learning backed by the science of reading.

I am LaChase, a reader and a leader. FastTrack Literacy, with your own version, JamDER+, was built with you in mind. It is here to speed up reading successes by giving you tools you can review, adapt, and shape for your class. Take it one pupil at a time, and together we will make literacy a shared journey. Come wid mi. Mik mi introduce you to mi friend Hooty Hoot.

Use the microphone in the CHEETAH® Reading Partner to let pupils dictate stories, check their reading levels, receive feedback, create their own stories, and more!

The CHEETAH® CAPE Tool

As you teach each sound, the lesson format will follow the CHEETAH® CAPE tool.

CONCEPT (exploration) sections give the information and knowledge the pupil needs to understand the lesson fully. Look at the letter that represents the phonic sound and practise making the sound together. Use the story and its action to hear the letter sound in context. Show the pupil where the phonic sound can appear in a word. Say the words in the word bank together and use the story to find more words with the focus sound.

> Teach me, and I will learn.

This symbol shows sections to be read by the adult. Using instruments and the CHEETAH® train song lyrics is another way for auditory learners to further explore the sound.

This icon in the My Tools section shows that a teacher or parent should help with the charts and activities.

APPLY (elaboration) The Apply section moves pupils initially from hearing a sound to actively using it through listening, identifying, and responding. Initial activities are auditory but begin the shift toward early sound-to-symbol understanding.

> Show me, and I will follow.

 The jingle symbol signals the Sing-and-Act routine, which reinforces the sound and prepares pupils for decoding.

 The pencil icon marks a short "write aloud" activity, where the teacher models saying each sound while writing and pupils mimic the process aloud.

PRACTICE (further elaboration) sections allow the pupil to use the information and skills they have learned during fun activities that are guided by the teacher.

Opportunities for collaborative practice and ICT-linked activities are marked with this symbol (⚙).

> Let me do it, and I will not forget.

EVALUATE (self-reflection) sections are a chance for the teacher and parent to communicate and keep track of the pupil's understanding of key concepts. Pupils get a chance to express their feelings. This is also where the pupil, parent or guardian will be given stickers to celebrate their learning!

How am I doing?

As with the generally held belief about reading, JamDER+ maintains that:

everyone can read

everyone can read and write.

Utilizing the simple and subtle approach of each pupil explaining what was learnt at school, we believe JamDER+ will not only teach a child but empower and educate adults in general and ultimately improve our nation's literacy rate.

Learn more about **JamDER+** offers on our CHEETAH® website www.mycheetahinc.com.

Welcome to **JamDER+**, a CHEETAH® Purrrrrrr Publishing production!

JamDER+,

building a nation one letter at a time.

List of JamDER+ Resources*

1. Teacher's Helper
2. Pupil's Helper
3. Phonics Big Book
4. Decodable & Early Readers (physical and digital books)
5. Decodable Poster Stories
6. Sentence strips
7. Sing and Act Songbook
8. My Own Words Bank
9. Interactive charts
10. Interactive videos
11. Apps
12. Digital curriculum (iCHEETAH© Educational Robot)
13. Digital images
14. Assessment tools:
    a. Fluency Tests
    b. Phonemic Awareness Daily Workout
    c. Phonics Assessment Sheet
15. Train the trainer sessions
16. National Literacy Competition

* Some items are sold separately.

How to Use Our Books

Books

✓ Teacher's Helper, Volumes 1 and 2

✓ Pupil's Helper, Volumes 1, 2 and 3

✓ C-DER® books

✓ Poster stories

Instead of using age labels, we use "Early Literacy Tool" on the front covers to avoid discouraging pupils whose reading levels may not match their ages, and to prevent parents from feeling disappointed about their child's current reading level. Refer to the list of JamDER+ resources for additional supplementary aids.

Prerequisites and Visual Aid

The My Tools section in the Teacher's Helper and Pupil's Books offers quick checks of prior learning and visual charts that summarise key letter-sound concepts. All charts appear in the teacher editions, while selected ones in the pupil books are included for adult guidance and home support.

What Each Set Contains

Every sound lesson for all nine sets follows a similar instructional pattern. Using Set 1 (/s/, short ă, /m/, short ĕ, /p/) as an example, each lesson has these components:

1. Review and rewards section
2. Song or call-and-response jingle
3. Sound discrimination, starting with the sound in the initial position
4. Teacher read-aloud #1 (listening only activity)
5. Picture activity (sound identification without print)
6. Letter formation and mouth cues
7. Teacher read-aloud #2 (short story)
8. My word wall (with singing and acting)
9. Word work mats (decoding + encoding)
10. Sight word activity

11. Decodable story ("I can read with you!" stories)
12. Self-assessment, parent/teacher notes and reward stickers
13. C-DER® book integration
14. CHEETAH® review
15. Practise (activities)
16. Supplementary resources
17. CHEETAH® Poster Fluency Tests.

Note: This structure repeats throughout the programme, and items 2, 3, 4, and 13 are not in the Pupil's Helper books. The pupil's book is intentionally simpler, so we do not overwhelm pupils; the Teacher's Helper carries the most difficult auditory stories and the fuller steps for guided instruction. Parents may skip item 4, and teachers may adjust by skipping, shortening, or reading the full story—depending on pupils' abilities.

See the attached "Suggested 65-Minute Teacher's Page" (one for each letter), which is prepared as a suggested guide for teachers and included in our training programme. Sets 1 to 4 are provided as supplemental resources. We will provide the link (digital access) to these resources.

How to use each section (step-by-step)

1. Review and rewards section

 Each letter begins with a review of the homework and prior lessons, plus cutting out and pasting reward stickers, when applicable, for parents and/or pupils.

2. Song or call-and-response jingle

Begin each lesson with the sound jingle and gesture. This part of the lesson is auditory only and uses call-and-response to engage pupils while training the ear before any print is shown. Instruction starts with the sound in the initial position only, with medial and final positions introduced later.

3. Sound discrimination starting with the sound in the initial position

 Pupils listen to words and decide whether the target sound is at the beginning, middle, or end, using pictures to support hearing rather than reading. Instructions are tiered with a focus on beginning letter sounds first. This builds strong phonemic awareness before introducing print, and some of the words come directly from the story in item 4 below.

4. Teacher read-aloud #1 (listening only activity)

Pupils listen for the target sound as the teacher reads a story aloud, for example, Sal the Seahorse. This is a listening exercise; there is no decoding or pointing, as this is strictly targeting phonemic awareness. The story can be used for differentiated learning for advanced readers.

5. Picture activity (sound identification without print)

Pupils will look at pictures while listening to the word associated with each picture and circle, draw lines, or complete other activities based on what they hear. This is mainly an auditory exercise.

6. Letter formation and mouth cues

The teacher will demonstrate how to shape the mouth for the phoneme while pupils' mimic. Pupils will also practise letter formation.

7. Teacher read-aloud #2 (short story)

This activity uses short, printed text, for example, Sam and the Sun, to help pupils connect the sound they have been hearing with the letter they now see. As they listen and then find the letter in the story, they learn that spoken sounds match written symbols. This step gently moves them from sound awareness into early reading, turning sound → symbol → word.

Additionally, Teachers will instruct pupils to underline, place a check mark, or add a dot under a specific letter-sound, then count and record the total. A blank space is provided at the end of each story for pupils to write this number. This activity also supports early mathematics by giving pupils practice in counting, comparing quantities, and recording simple numerical information.

8. My word wall (with singing and acting)

The jingle/action symbol signals the shift into early word recognition. This is used alongside the CHEETAH® Sing and Act Songbook which provides the lyrics of and the actions to songs written to reinforce each letter sound. Pupils will sing along and carry out the prescribed action.

The word wall section promotes vocabulary development by highlighting the word of the day in a gold star shape. The word of the day reinforces the letter sound being taught.

9. Word work mats (decoding + encoding)

Word Work Mats are structured practice sheets that help pupils connect the taught sound to letters and simple words, supporting early spelling and reading development. This is the structured decoding sequence:

- say and tap
- map
- graph
- check
- write

This is where true decoding and spelling routines begin and the concept "write aloud" is introduced and practised. Teachers assign the words for this exercise and guide pupils to say each decoding step aloud as they write. For example, they name each sound, blend it, and then write the whole word. This mat can be used as a big interactive chart for collaborative classroom work.

10. Sight word activity

Sight words are introduced for recognition rather than decoding, since many cannot be sounded out easily. Pupils practise speaking, reading and using them in simple sentences so they become fluent readers. This activity also helps pupils become familiar with the sight words before they encounter them in the group reading story.

11. Decodable story ("I can read with you!" stories)

Pupils decode the controlled text for the sound taught, and many of the words in this story also appear on the My Word Wall. The teacher first reads the story aloud, and then the class reads it together as a group activity. The teacher guides pupils through the comprehension questions and may call on individuals to answer specific questions. The goal is for pupils to ultimately read the story accurately, fluently and with comprehension.

Access to the CHEETAH Reading Partner (Literacy GPT) is included in the Practise section to support differentiated learning. This allows teachers to check reading levels and create personalised stories.

12. Self-reflection, parent/teacher notes and reward stickers

Pupils are encouraged to reflect on and assess their progress by selecting "Got it, Almost Got It / or Didn't get it." Teachers and parents provide feedback by signing the included evaluation form for mastery tracking.

13. C-DER® book integration

The C-DER® series (At the Farm, Meet My Family, Mr. Pete Makes Friends, etc.) is a required part of every sound lesson and serves three purposes: cementing the reading–writing connection, serving as homework assignments and providing review opportunities.

A. Cementing the reading–writing connection by introducing a C-DER® book at the end of a lesson. At the end of each 65-minute lesson, teachers may say, for example, "Tonight, read C-DER® book ___. Find the words with the sound __."

Note that although each book is officially assigned to a letter, it may also be used to support additional letter-sound patterns. Some books are not tied to any specific letter sound at all but are instead designed for fluency practice and for building recognition of word families.

Pupils will:

- read the book with support
- hunt for target-sound words
- bring one written/drawn sentence or a teacher-assigned activity to the next class.

Before you begin reading, use the book to introduce the literacy title and author. During the story, point to a character(s) on the cover and ask, "Who is this character?" and "What do you think this story is about?" After the story, discuss, "What is this story about?" "Can you retell the story in your storyteller's voice?" These questions are great for text-to-self, text-to-the-world and text-to-text.

B. C-DER® homework assignments

Whether pupils access the C-DER® books at home or school—physically or through an app—they can be assigned homework to reinforce learning. Pupils re-read the story with a parent or guardian, highlight or list target-sound words, and provide evidence of reading. Evidence may include an oral summary, a picture, or a written sentence, depending on the teacher's instructions. Assigning C-DER® books as homework facilitates:

- home–school link
- daily decoding practice
- repetition with controlled text.

C. Daily drill activities

Each day, teachers will take 5–7 minutes to do the daily review and warm-up routine. Teachers may:

- revisit 2–3 sentences from the C-DER® book assigned the night before
- check for accuracy, sound mastery, fluency and expression
- review new words learned
- quickly test blending and decoding using words from the book.

This builds consistency:

- yesterday: C-DER® assigned
- today: C-DER® reviewed
- throughout: sounds reinforced through familiar text

This forms a tight loop: teach → assign → revisit → consolidate.

Why C-DER® books integration works

i. Sound-first instruction is foundational. Children must hear a phoneme before mapping it to print.

ii. Repeated exposure in predictable text accelerates mastery. C-DER® books use sight words, CVC patterns, familiar characters and controlled vocabulary.

iii. Revisiting text the next day moves words into long-term memory. This creates orthographic mapping through spaced repetition.

iv. Daily drill links yesterday's learning with today's lesson. This reduces forgetting and builds fluency.

v. Home reading extends instructional minutes. Reading at home expands the learning day far beyond the 65-minute classroom block.

14. CHEETAH Review

The CHEETAH® review pages provide quick consolidation at the end of each set of letters. Pupils revisit the sound through mixed activities—listening, marking, building and reading—to confirm mastery before moving on. While repetition in the picture activity creates the consistent pattern needed for sound recognition and for the upcoming app, the review pages balance this by offering a wider variety of engaging tasks.

Teachers may choose to use some or all of the activities. Some sections can be used for group activities or as solo tests and may be a great way to gauge pupils' understanding.

15. Practise (activities)

The Practise section gives pupils fun, hands-on opportunities to extend what they have learned. Activities vary by sound and may include simple crafts, group tasks, ICT-linked activities, or using iCHEETAH© to create or record short responses. These tasks strengthen understanding by letting children explore the sound in practical, playful ways guided by the teacher.

16. Supplementary resources

Flash cards, charts, tools, assessment sheets, the iCHEETAH© and other resources are useful aids that will make learning fun and speed up reading successes.

17. Fluency Tests

The Fluency Tests in this book are progressive and restrictive. They are progressive because each new test builds gently on the sounds and words pupils have already learned, so the stories become a little longer and more complex over time. They are restrictive because every test uses only the letters and patterns that have been taught so far, with no surprises or unknown spellings. This way, pupils can focus on reading more accurately and quickly, while teachers can be sure they are testing true fluency, not guesswork.

This brief guide introduces the core ideas, but much more awaits you. You can access extended resources anytime through our resource link, and our training sessions will offer deeper support. I'm here as your wise owl, ready to help you master each lesson.

I Can Read!

Test me!

Pet on the Mat

Sam met Pam by the mat.	6
Pam sat on the mat with Sam.	13
A pet ran to Pam and Sam.	20
The pet sat on the mat by Sam.	28
Have a sip, Pam.	32
Can the pet sip it?	37
The pet can tip it!	42
Nip the mat!	45
Rip!	46
The pet gave Pam the tin.	52
The pet had a nap on the mat	60
by Pam and Sam.	64

Comprehension check:

1. Who sat on the mat?

2. What did the pet give Pam?

3. Why do you think the pet took a nap?

My Reading Record

Reading #1: ____ WCPM
Reading #2: ____ WCPM
Reading #3: ____ WCPM

Suggested Advice to Pupils and Parents

Before you began the JamDER+ Reading Test, we wanted to understand what you already knew about sounds, words, and reading. This check was not a race and it was not officially graded. It simply helped us see the skills you were ready to learn next. You read each part carefully, tried your best, and showed us your starting point for the journey ahead.

We were proud of the effort you gave, and we knew you were ready to grow even stronger as a reader. Ready to go on a learning adventure? Let's go!

My Tools

Jamaican Decodable & Early Readers

Phonics Chart*

Set 1 — s, short ă, m, short ĕ, p

Set 2 — f, n, short ĭ, t, r

Set 3 — d, short ŏ, hard g, h, k

Set 4 — l, b, short ŭ, soft g, long ā

Set 5 — j, long ī, or, long ō, z

Set 6 — ng, w/wh, short oo, long oo, v

Set 7 — ch, sh, long ē, th, y

Set 8 — x, qu, oi, long ū, ar

Set 9 — ow, ou, er, zh

Bonus letter sound: soft c

*As provided by the Ministry of Education, Skills, Youth and Information

8 + 1 Steps to Reading

ADULT HELP

1 — I want to learn to read!
✔ Reading, and understanding what I read, helps me to learn new things and use my imagination.

2 — I know all my letters!
✔ Name each letter (a to z – the alphabet)
✔ Name the vowels (a, e, i, o, u)
✔ Name the consonants (b, c, d, f, g, h, j, k, l, m, n, p, q, r, s, t, v, w, x, y, z)
✔ Say the sound that goes with each letter (for example, m says /m/)
✔ Point to a letter when I hear its sound
✔ Switch a sound: sat ⟶ change /s/ to /m/ ⟶ mat

3 — I have magic ears to:
✔ Hear each sound in a word
✔ Find words that sound alike (cat / hat)
✔ Count the words in a sentence (for example, I / am / Sam = 3 words)

4 — I can build (blend) and break (segment) words into sounds!
✔ Build the word: /s/ + /a/ + /t/ ⟶ sat
✔ Break the word apart: sat ⟶ /s/ /a/ /t/
✔ Work on the Word Work Mat (see the chart in this book):
  • Say and tap the word – one tap for each sound
  • Count the number of sounds I hear
  • Write the matching letter for each sound I hear
  • Compare the number of sounds with the number of letters in the word

19

5 — I can write my letters, words, and sentences the correct way!

- ✓ Write big (uppercase or capital) letters
- ✓ Write small (lowercase) letters
- ✓ Say the sound while I air-write each letter
- ✓ Say the sound while I finger-trace each letter
- ✓ Say the sound while I write each letter on paper
- ✓ Write words
- ✓ Write sentences

6 — I know the tricky or sight words!

- ✓ Read words like the, was, said
- ✓ Sound out what I can in each word
- ✓ Notice the tricky part that doesn't follow the rules

7 — I can sound out, spell, and write 2-, 3-, and 4-letter words!

- ✓ 2-letter (CV syllables): for example, ba, pe, to
- ✓ 3-letter (CVC words): for example, bat, pet, top
- ✓ Word families: for example, cat, nap, sad
- ✓ 4-letter words: for example, cane, make (magic e), rain (ai)

8 — I can read little sentences and books!

- ✓ Read once for awareness
- ✓ Read a second time for accuracy
- ✓ Read a third time for fluency and comprehension – in my storyteller's voice

+1 — I will grow and show my reading skills!

- ✓ I can share what I have learnt with my parents, friends, or teacher.

The Alphabet

Aa Bb Cc Dd Ee

Ff Gg Hh Ii Jj

Kk Ll Mm Nn Oo

Pp Qq Rr Ss Tt

Uu Vv Ww Xx Yy

Zz

Do you know all the letters?

The Alphabet

Aa Bb Cc Dd

Ee Ff Gg Hh

Ii Jj Kk Ll

Mm Nn Oo Pp

Qq Rr Ss Tt

Uu Vv Ww Xx

Yy Zz

Jamaican Decodable & Early Readers

Alphabet Test 1

(Fill-in Edition)

Say each pair of letters aloud and write the missing ones in the boxes. Match the same case (capital and lowercase).

Aa Bb ☐☐ Dd

Ee ☐☐ Gg Hh

☐☐ Jj ☐☐ Ll

Mm ☐☐ Oo ☐☐

Qq Rr ☐☐

☐☐ Vv Ww

Xx ☐☐ Zz

Alphabet Test 2

When I say 'begin', start and tell me the names of the letters as fast as you can. If you don't know one, I'll tell you. Keep going until I say 'stop'.

🟢 Start Here

p	d	V	K	D	K	T	o	R	d
d	y	k	T	O	u	V	q	m	z
g	S	b	P	K	G	q	w	V	w
C	t	G	E	Q	v	V	U	h	e
H	X	X	r	J	I	v	C	N	r
v	n	E	B	j	F	M	I	P	N
o	f	z	J	Z	X	V	i	E	A
D	I	f	u	n	F	i	u	c	j
Z	O	O	m	a	W	M	s	h	d
t	q	Y	H	x	r	Z	L	t	H

✓ Correct: ＿＿＿＿   Ø Errors: ＿＿＿＿   Final Score: ＿＿＿＿

24

Short Vowels

ă	ĕ	ĭ	ŏ	ŭ
ant 	hen 	sit 	dog 	bus 
apple 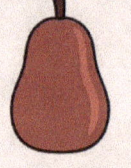	pen 	tin 	box 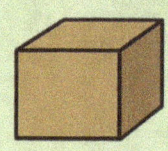	sun 
map 	bed 	pig 	pot 	cup 
cat 	vet 	insect 	jog 	rug 

Blend Two Sounds

Vowels → Consonants ↓	a	e	i	o	u
b	ba	be	bi	bo	bu
c	ca	ce	ci	co	cu
d	da	de	di	do	du
f	fa	fe	fi	fo	fu
g	ga	ge	gi	go	gu
h	ha	he	hi	ho	hu
j	ja	je	ji	jo	ju
k	ka	ke	ki	ko	ku
l	la	le	li	lo	lu
m	ma	me	mi	mo	mu
n	na	ne	ni	no	nu
p	pa	pe	pi	po	pu
qu	qua	que	qui	quo	qu
r	ra	re	ri	ro	ru
s	sa	se	si	so	su
t	ta	te	ti	to	tu
v	va	ve	vi	vo	vu
w	wa	we	wi	wo	wu
x	xa	xe	xi	xo	xu
z	za	ze	zi	zo	zu

Can you hear the sound, the sound?

Word Families
short ă

ăd	ăg	ăm	ăn	ăp	ăr	ăt	ăw	ăy
bad	bag	ham	can	cap	bar	bat	jaw	bay
dad	gag	jam	man	lap	car	cat	law	day
had	lag	tam	pan	map	far	fat	paw	lay
lad	nag	yam	ran	nap	jar	hat	raw	may
mad	rag		tan	pap	tar	mat	saw	pay
pad	tag		van	tap	war	rat		ray
sad				zap		sat		say
wad						tat		way

The better you read,
the more you see!

Word Families

short ĕ

ĕb	ĕd	ĕg	ĕn	ĕp	ĕt
web	bed	beg	den	pep	bet
	fed	keg	men	step	get
	led	leg	pen		jet
	red	peg	ten		let
	wed		hen		met
					net
					pet
					set
					vet
					wet
					yet

Letters make words, and words make you strong!

Jamaican Decodable & Early Readers

Word Families

short ĭ

ĭb	ĭd	ĭg	ĭm	ĭn	ĭp	ĭt
bib	bid	big	dim	bin	dip	bit
rib	did	dig	him	fin	hip	fit
	lid	fig	rim	pin	lip	hit
	kid	gig		tin	nip	kit
		pig		win	rip	lit
		wig			sip	pit
					tip	sit
					zip	

Every sound you blend is a step ahead!

Word Families

short ŏ

ŏb	ŏd	ŏg	ŏm	ŏn	ŏp	ŏt	ŏx	ŏw	ŏy
cob	cod	dog	mom	son	cop	cot	box	bow	boy
job	god	fog	Tom	ton	hop	dot	fox	cow	joy
mob	nod	hog			mop	got	ox	how	toy
rob	pod	log			pop	hot		now	
sob	rod	jog			top	lot		row	
	sod	bog				not		sow	
						pot			

I am Hooty Hoot, the wise Jamaican owl.

LaChase and I are good friends. Together we will educate, entertain and inspire you.

Mek wi fly into reading!

Word Families

short ŭ

ŭb	ŭd	ŭg	ŭm	ŭn	ŭp	ŭs
cub	bud	bug	gum	bun	cup	bus
hub	mud	hug	hum	fun	pup	us
rub	dud	jug	sum	gun	sup	
sub		lug		nun	up	
tub		mug		run		
		rug		sun		
		tug				

Run with the sounds, leap with the words!

31

Jamaican **D**ecodable **&** Early **R**eaders

Word Work Mat

Say & tap · Map (sounds) · Graph (letters) · Check · Write it

Say it & tap it					
Map it					
Graph it					
Check it	Sound			Letter	
Write it					

Say it & tap it					
Map it					
Graph it					
Check it	Sound			Lette	
Write it					

> Put a ♥ above any part of the word that is tricky.

*Adapted and modified by CHEETAH Toys & More, LLC for inclusion in this educational work.

32

Dolch Sight Words

(133 Pre-Primer to Grade 1*)

I	black	four	how	my	put	that	we
a	blue	from	in	new	ran	the	well
after	brown	funny	into	no	red	them	went
again	but	get	is	not	ride	then	were
all	by	give	it	now	round	there	what
am	came	go	jump	of	run	they	when
an	can	going	just	old	said	think	where
and	come	good	know	on	saw	this	white
any	could	had	let	once	say	three	who
are	did	has	like	one	see	to	will
as	do	have	little	open	she	too	with
ask	down	he	live	our	so	two	yellow
at	eat	help	look	out	some	under	yes
ate	every	her	make	over	soon	up	you
away	find	here	may	play	stop	walk	
be	fly	him	me	please	take	want	
big	for	his	must	pretty	thank	was	

* Adapted for educational purposes

. stop

! wow

? ask

read with me!

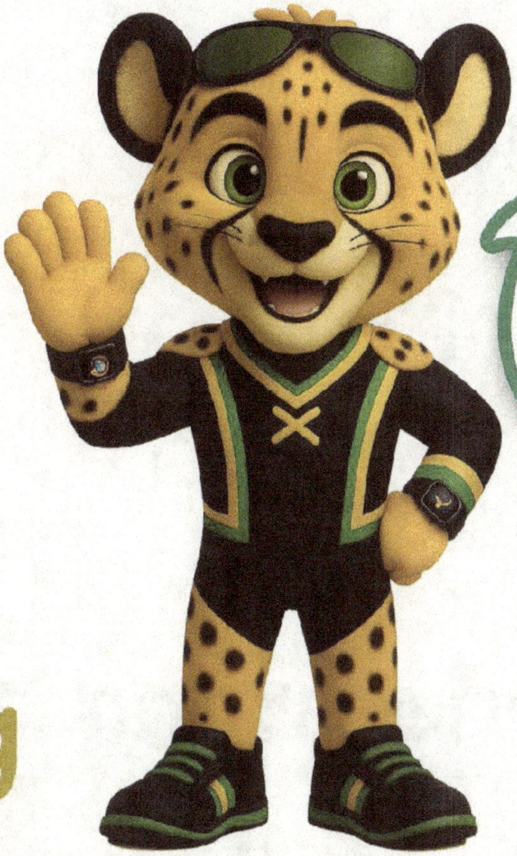

" " talking voice

, pause

1. 👂 Hear it

2. 👁 See it

3. 👄 Say it

4. ✏️ Write it

5. 📖 Read it

6. 💡 Understand it

7. 🧒 Share it

Set 1: s, short ă, m, short ĕ and p

Please refer to the relevant Poster Stories to be used with this set's focus sounds. In addition, here are the recommended C-DER® books to be used for comprehension instruction:

Sound	C-DER® reference	Book title
s	Set 1, Book 1	At the Farm
short ă	Set 1, Book 2	Meet My Family
m	Set 1, Book 3 and 1	Mr Pete Makes Friends At the Farm (read again)
short ĕ	Set 1, Book 4 and 5	Off to the Vet Play Time with My Friends
p	Set 1, Books 6, 8 and 1	House Flood Fun with My Doll At the Farm (read again)

Teaching tips*:

- Make sure the /s/ sound is pure 'ssss' rather than /z/ or 'suh.'
- the short ă sound is pronounced 'a' as in 'cat.'
- make sure the /m/ sound is pure 'mmmm' rather than 'muh.'
- the short ĕ sound is pronounced 'eh' as in 'egg.'
- the /p/ sound involves no vocalization. It is pronounced by keeping the lips tightly together and teeth apart, pursing the lips and pushing out the air.

Other useful CHEETAH® resources:

- CVC puzzles
- tricky words cards
- letters
- songs

Wah gwaan? My name is Hooty Hoot. LaChase and I are friends. I am here to guide you to the highest heights in reading. Let's soar together!

*Please see the appendices and Pupil's Helper for additional tips.

The /s/ sound

Let us read book 1,
At the Farm.

 CHEETAH® train loves a song, zooming as it hums along.
It zooms beside the sea, past a seal swimming free.
Can you guess which sound is next?

Find an instrument, then play and sing along using the lyrics above!

Use your mouth to make my sound!

The /s/ sound is on the way to town.
The CHEETAH® train is slowing down.

Concept: phonic sound /s/

Ss

The /s/ sound can appear at the start, in the middle or at the end of a word.

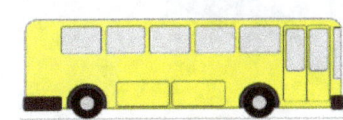

saw	insect	bus
said	messy	yes
see	inside	gas

Sal the Seahorse

Sal was a seahorse who lived in the sea. One Sunday he built a sandcastle the size of a bus. It was so big Sue the Seal saw it from six miles away.

"Is this your house?" said Sue.

"Yes," said Sal. "Please, come and see inside."

As they went to sit on a soft sofa, they heard a loud sound from outside. It was a tornado and it began to blow the sand away.

"It is not safe here," said Sal, running as quickly as he could. "It is safer in the sea!"

38

Apply: /s/

Listen to the word for each picture. (Circle) the picture if you hear the /s/ sound.

Practise writing the letter *s*.

Keep your teeth together and let the air slide out. Splendid!

Listen to the story. (Circle) the letter S or s if you hear the sound.

Sam and the Sun!

Mrs. Sun says, "Hello, Sam!"

So, Sam stops to share some stories.

At sunset, they say their sweet goodbyes.

"See you soon Mrs. Sun!"

/s/ sound = _____

My Word Wall

Ss

(from the story *Sam and Pam*)

Sam	sat	see	said
I	am	sun	on
and	a	look	at
	the	had	do	
Pam	sat	mat	you

Colour the words that you know.
You are a super reader!

My Word Work Mats*

Say & tap · Map (sounds) · Graph (letters) · Check · Write it

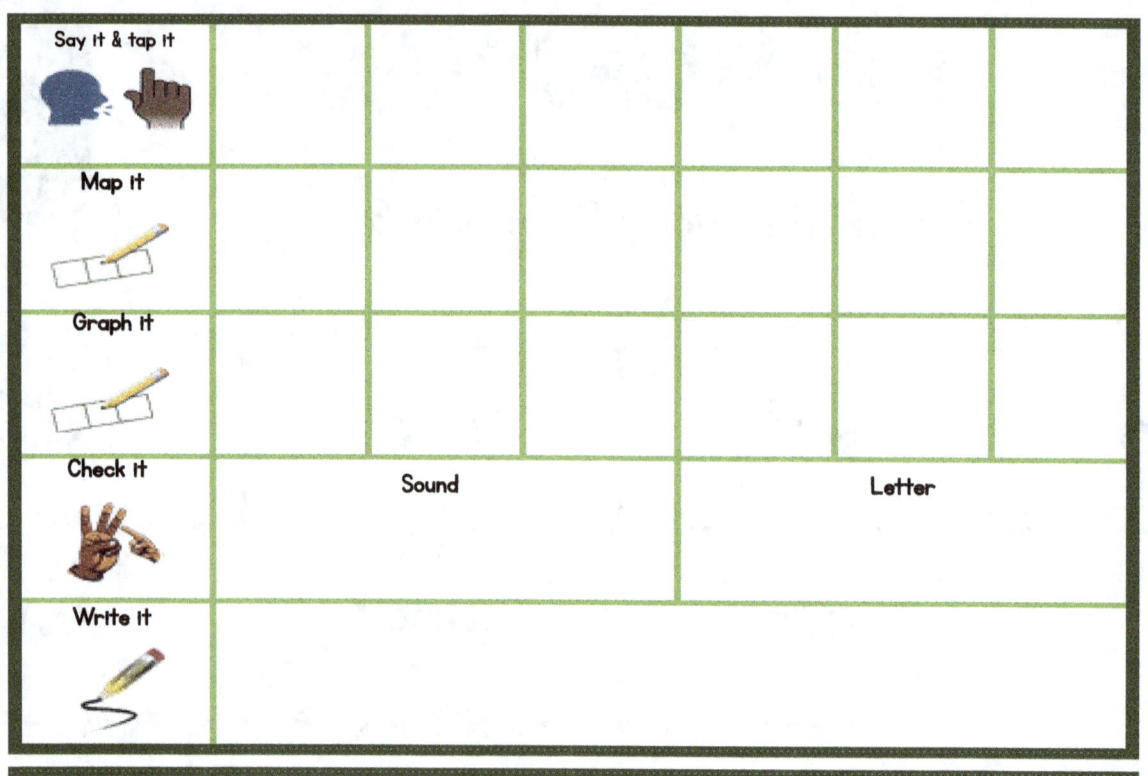

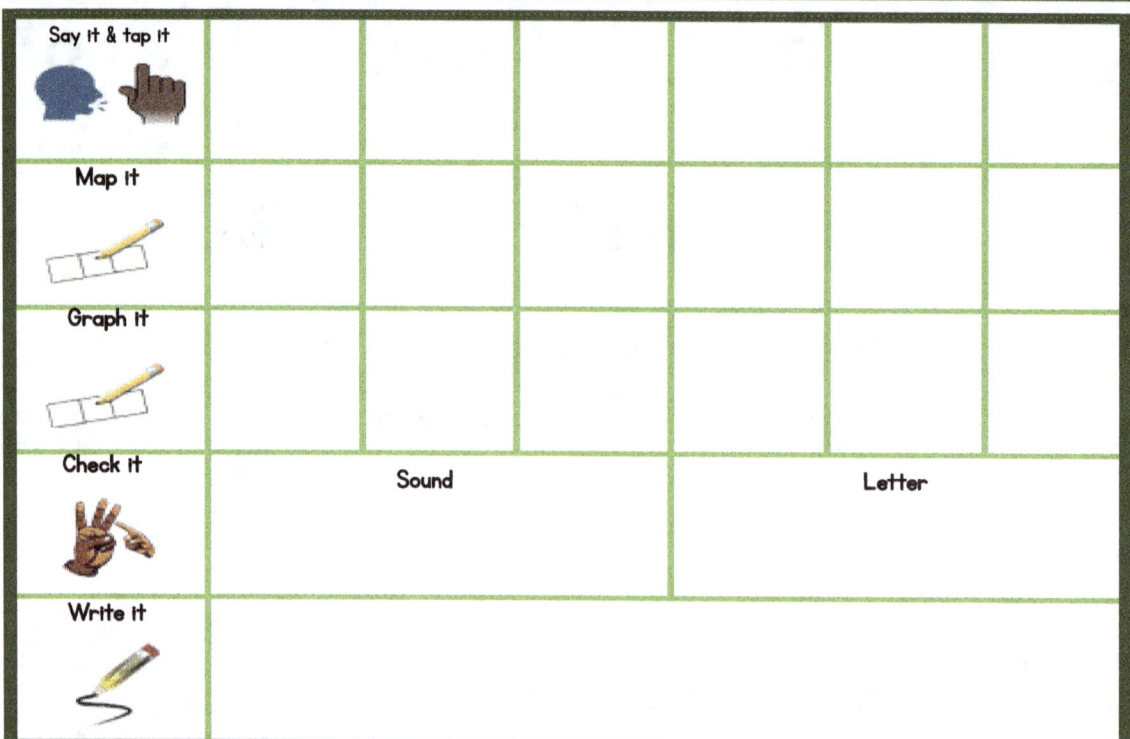

Learn more words from C-DER book I, *At the Farm*. Use your Word Families poster in My Tools section ("poster") to learn **-am** and **-at** words.

Put a ♥ above any part of the word that is tricky.

*Adapted and modified by CHEETAH® Toys & More, LLC for inclusion in this educational work.

Sight Words Activity

(words I see all the time)

Your teacher will say each word.

Put a check mark (✓) beside each word.

☐ I	☐ at
☐ am	☐ the
☐ said	☐ had
☐ and	☐ do
☐ on	☐ you
☐ a	☐ see
☐ look	

Sentences:

1. I am Pam

2. Sam sat on a mat

I can read with y

Name: _____

Sam Sit

"I am Sam," said Sam.

Pam said, "I am Pam."

Pam and Sam sat on a mat.

Pam said, "Look at the map."

Pam and Sam had a map on the mat.

Practise: /s/

Mould playdough into a sausage and bend it into the letter *s*.

Use pebbles, buttons, or any other small objects to make the shape of the letter *s*.

Reread the C-DER® book, *At the Farm*. Group the /s/ words from the story according to where the sound appears in the word.

Use a sock to make a snake puppet that hisses.

Ask the CHEETAH Reading Partner© to make a silly short story using sun and sand.

Classroom Action: Teacher reads the story aloud. Pupils hiss softly each time they hear the /s/ sound.

Evaluate: /s/

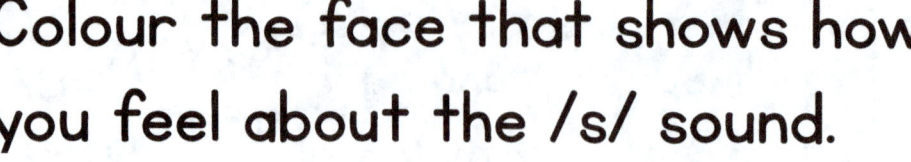

Colour the face that shows how you feel about the /s/ sound.

Are you ready to find out what sound is next? Then let's fly!

Got it!

Almost got it

No, didn't get it

Dear Parent: Date: _____

_____ does/does not fully understand the phonic sound /s/. Please continue to review at home.

Signed: _____

Dear Teacher: Date: _____

Thank you. We have reviewed the phonic sound /s/ together. My child had a chance to teach me.

Signed: _____

Reward sticker for parent or guardian goes here.

Well done!

Sticker for pupil goes here!

_____

(write name here)

understands the phonic sound /s/.

45

Let us read book 2,
Meet My Family.

CHEETAH® train loves a song, zooming as it hums along.
It zooms across the street. Oh, angry ants are on the seat.
Can you guess which sound is next?

> Find an instrument, then play and sing along using the lyrics above!

> Can you make my sound three times?

The short ă sound is on the way to town.
The CHEETAH® train is slowing down.

Concept: phonic sound short ă

The short ă sound can appear at the start or in the middle of a word.

Aa

ant
and
am

can
has
family

Alan the Astronaut

Alan the astronaut could not stop eating. Alan had already eaten a lot of avocados. Next, he jumped around like an acrobat onto a plate of apple pies. Soon Alan's belly began to ache. "Ahh," said Alan, rubbing his tummy.
"You have eaten too much!" said Sam.
"And look at that mess across the table!" Sam put on an apron.
"I will clean it up while you have a nap," he said.
Soon Alan was sleeping and snoring like a cat. When Alan awoke, he was feeling much better.
"Thank you for caring for me, Sam," said Alan.

Apply: short ă

Listen to the word for each picture. Colour the picture if you hear the short ă sound.

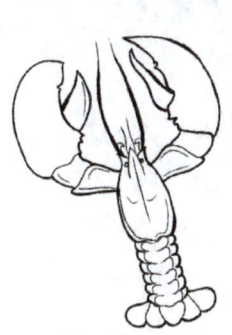

Practise writing the letter a.

Open wide and say /ă/ like you're surprised. Amazing!

Listen to the story. <u>Underline</u> the letter A or a if you hear the short ă sound.

Anna the Ant

"I am an ant," says Anna the ant.

Anna has an apple.

The apple is as big as Anna!

Anna says, "Can ant eat apples?"

"We can eat an apple a day," the ants say.

short ă sound = _____

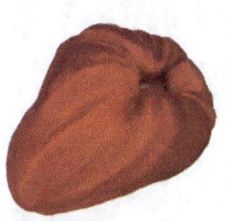

48

My Word Wall

(from the story *Sam and the Ant*)

ant	Ann	and	Sam

on	is	saw

to	in	mat

an	sat

Colour the words you know.
You always aim high!

JamDER+
Jamaican Decodable & Early Readers

My Word Work Mats*

Say & tap · Map (sounds) · Graph (letters) · Check · Write it

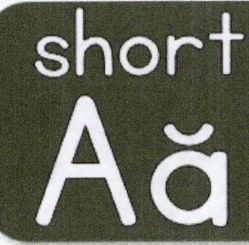

short

Aă

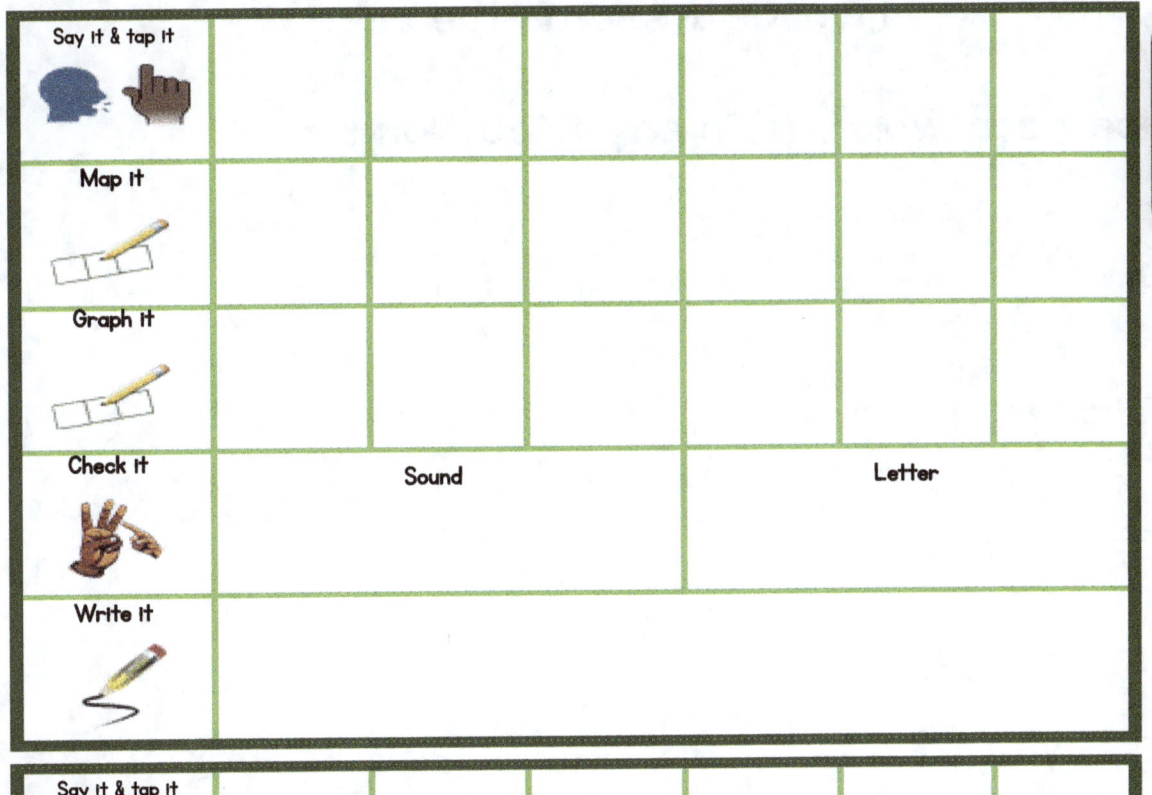

Say It & tap It				
Map It				
Graph It				
Check It	Sound		Letter	
Write It				

Say It & tap It				
Map It				
Graph It				
Check It	Sound		Letter	
Write It				

Put a ♥ above any part of the word that is tricky.

Get more words from C-DER® book 2, *Meet My Family*. Review your poster for **-am** and **-at** word families.

*Adapted and modified by CHEETAH® Toys & More, LLC for inclusion in this educational work.

Sight Words Activity

(words I see all the time)

Trace each word, then say it out loud.

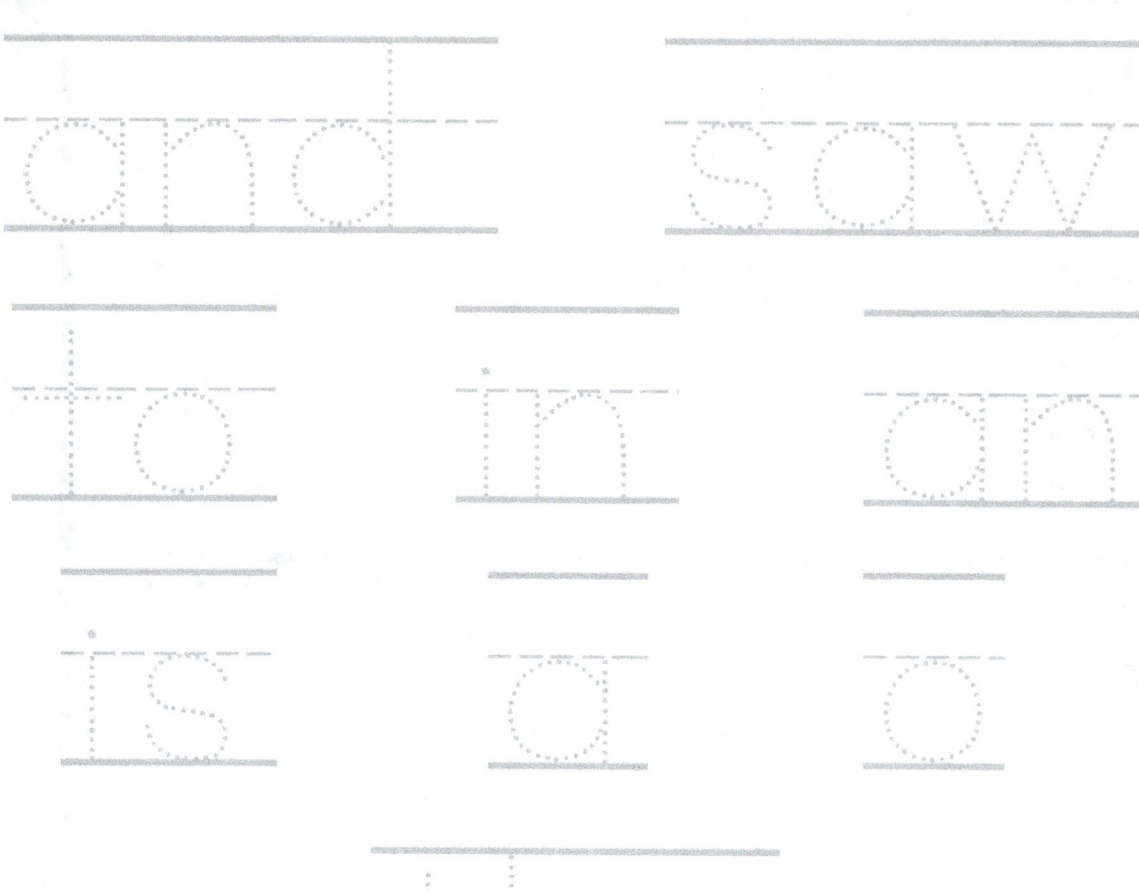

and   saw

to   in   an

is   a   o

the

Sentences:

1. Sam sat.

2. Pam ran.

I can read with you!

short Aă

Name: _____

Sam and the Ant

Sam sat on a mat.
The pan is on the mat.
Sam saw an ant.
Ann the ant ran to the pan.
The ant sat in the pan.
Sam and the ant sat.

Answer these questions:

1. What happened first in the story?

2. Can you retell the story as a storyteller?

3. What happened at the end of the story?

My Reading Record

Reading #1: ____ WCPM
Reading #2: ____ WCPM
Reading #3: ____ WCPM

Practise: short ă

Use the CVC letter pieces to build words with the short ă in the middle.

As part of a group, play *Pass the Hat*.
Fill the hat with CVC words and take turns to pull one out. If it contains a short ă word, keep the card.

Paint the letter *a* and draw pictures that begin with the short ă around it.

Reread the *C-DER®* book, *Meet my Family*. Collect the short ă sight words flashcards that appear in the story. Practise reading them.

Use the iCHEETAH© to record yourself reading the *Anna the Ant* story in this lesson.

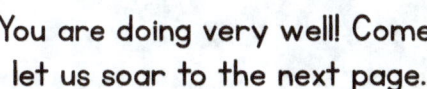

Evaluate: short ă

Colour the face that shows how you feel about the short ă sound.

Got it!

Almost got it

No, didn't get it

You are doing very well! Come, let us soar to the next page.

Dear Parent: Date: _____

_____ does/does not fully understand the phonic sound short ă. Please continue to review at home.

Signed: _____

Dear Teacher: Date: _____

Thank you. We have reviewed the phonic sound short ă together. My child had a chance to teach me.

Signed: _____

Reward sticker for parent or guardian goes here.

Well done!

_____
(write name here)

understands the phonic sound short ă.

Sticker for pupil goes here!

Mr. Pete Makes Friends
At the Farm

The /m/ sound

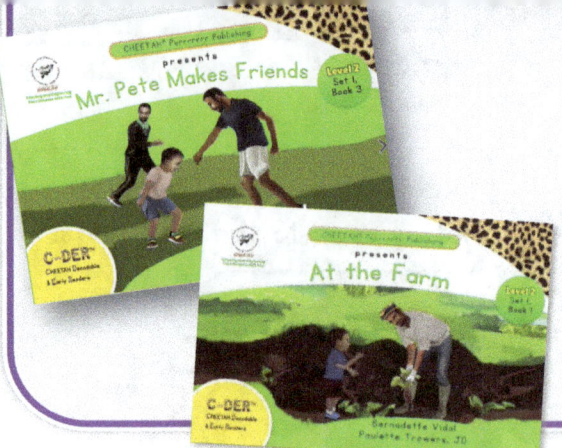

Let us read books 1, *At the Farm* (read again), and 3, *Mr. Pete Makes Friends.*

CHEETAH® train loves a song, zooming as it hums along.
It zooms across the map, while Monkey Mike takes a nap.
Can you guess which letter sound is next?

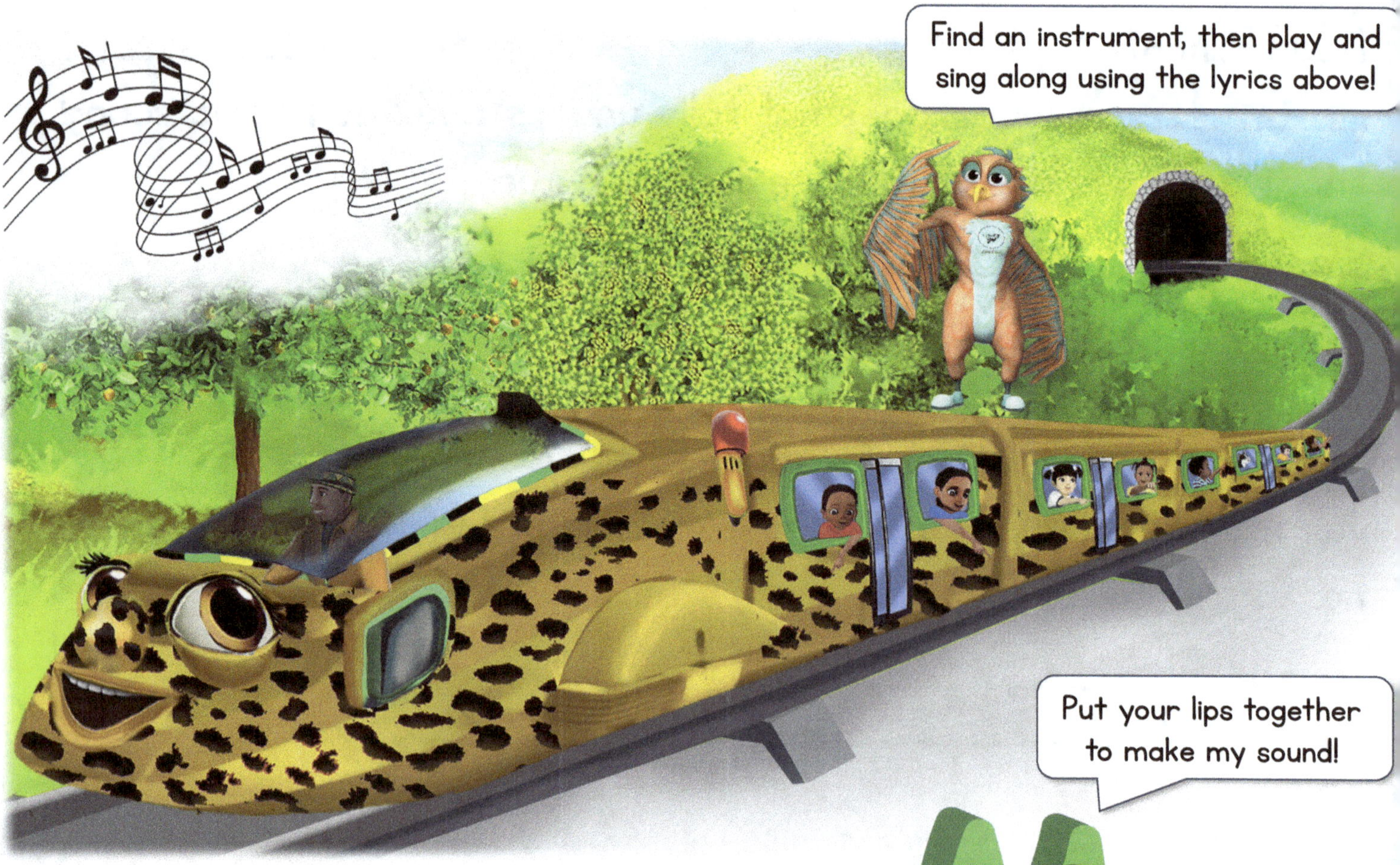
Find an instrument, then play and sing along using the lyrics above!

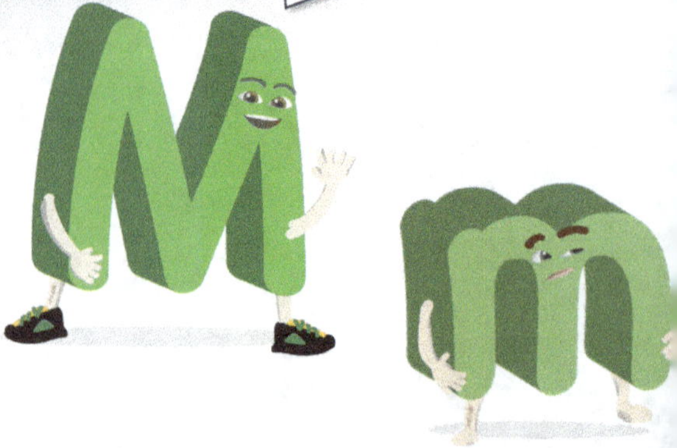
Put your lips together to make my sound!

The /m/ sound is on the way to town.
The CHEETAH® train is slowing down.

Concept: phonic sound /m/

The /m/ sound can appear at the start, in the middle or at the end of a word.

Mm

man   woman   drum

me   tomato   him

make   lemon   them

Monkey Mike

Mike the monkey travelled to Montego Bay from Mexico. "Mmmm," he mumbled. "My memory is not amazing!"

"May I help you?" Sam asked him. Sam was eating a mango.

"I am in a muddle," said Mike.

"I left my passport under my mattress!"

"Oh dear me!" said Sam, as Mike leaped into the sea.

"It is okay. My mom made a submarine at the marina. I will pilot it back to Mexico in minutes!"

"Mmmm," mumbled Sam. "If your memory is so bad, maybe I should make you a map!"

Apply: /m/

Listen to the words for each picture. (Circle) the pictures if you hear the /m/ sound.

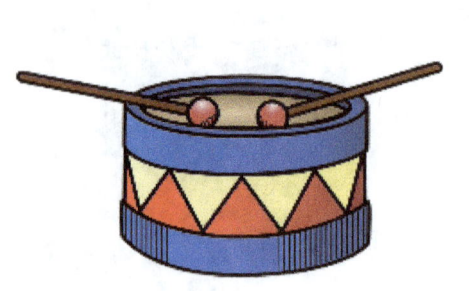

Practise writing the letter *m*.

Press your lips together and hum

Great job!

Listen to the story. Add a √ above the letter M or m if you hear the /m/ sound.

My Map

Mike is a monkey with many maps.

The map shows Mike Jamaica.

He follows some mountains.

"Mike! Use your map. Don't miss the mark!"

/m/ sound = _____

My Word Wall

(from the story *The Map*)

man	map	mat	pam

ham	with	come

said	had	saw	and

ate	then	they

Colour the words you know.
You always aim high!

My Word Work Mats*

Say & tap · Map (sounds) · Graph (letters) · Check · Write it

Mn

Say it & tap it						
Map it						
Graph it						
Check it	Sound				Letter	
Write it						

Say it & tap it					
Map it					
Graph it					
Check it	Sound			Letter	
Write it					

Put a ♥ above any part of the word that is tricky.

Get more words from C-DER® books 1, *At the Farm*, again and 3, *Mr. Pete Makes Friends*. Review the **-ap** and **-am** word families.

*Adapted and modified by CHEETAH® Toys & More, LLC for inclusion in this educational work.

JamDER+
Jamaican Decodable & Early Readers

Sight Words Activity

Take turns doing a spelling test with a partner. One person says the word, and the other person writes it.

saw _____   had _____

with _____   in _____

come ____   and _____

on _____   ate _____

said _____   then ____

the _____   they ____

Sentences:

1. Sam saw Pam.

2. The man sat.

I can read with you!

Mm

Name: _____

The Map

Sam saw a man with a map.

"Come sit on the mat," said Sam.

The man sat on the mat.

The man had ham in a bag.

Pam saw Sam and the man.

Sam, Pam, and the man ate ham.

Then they sat with the map.

Answer these questions:

My Reading Record

Reading #1: _____ WCPM
Reading #2: _____ WCPM
Reading #3: _____ WCPM

1. What happened first in the story?

2. Can you retell the story as a storyteller?

3. What happened at the end of the story?

March around the room, making an mmmm sound at the people you pass.

Make a monster by gluing eyes and teeth onto the letter M.

Reread the C-DER® book, *Mr. Pete Makes Friends*. Make a list of all the words in the story that have the /m/ sound.

Prompt:

Tell iCHEETAH©, to create a story about a monkey and some mangoes.

Classroom Action:
As iCHEETAH© tells the story, pupils hum softly ("mmm…") each time they hear a word beginning with the /m/ sound.

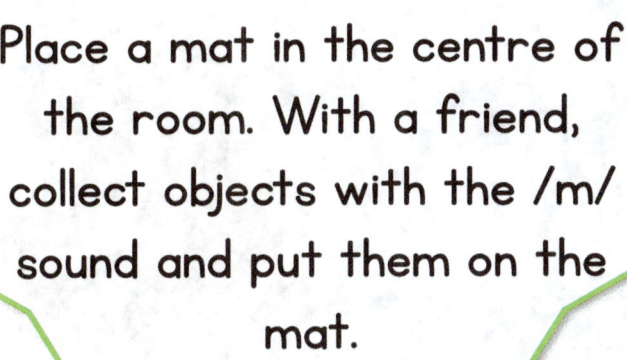

Place a mat in the centre of the room. With a friend, collect objects with the /m/ sound and put them on the mat.

Use blue to colour Montego Bay on a map of Jamaica. Colour the mountains green.

Evaluate: /m/

Colour the face that shows how you feel about the /m/ sound.

Got it!

Almost got it

No, didn't get it

Dear Parent: Date: _____

_____ does/does not fully understand the phonic sound /m/. Please continue to review at home.

Signed: _____

Dear Teacher: Date: _____

Thank you. We have reviewed the phonic sound /m/ together. My child had a chance to teach me.

Signed: _____

Reward sticker for parent or guardian goes here.

Well done!

_____

(write name here)

understands the phonic sound /m/.

Sticker for pupil goes here!

Off to the Vet
Play Time with My Friends

The short ĕ sound

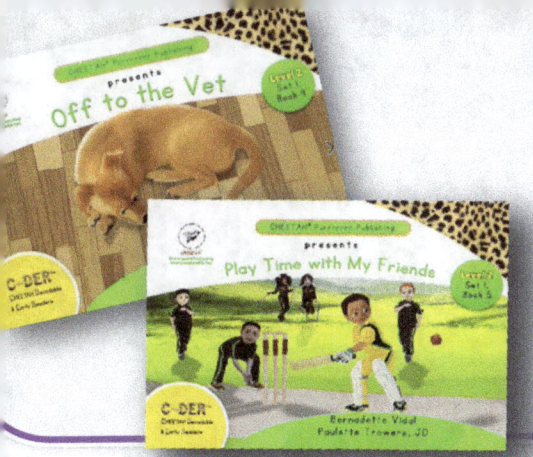

Let us read books 4, *Off to the Vet*, and 5, *Play Time with My Friends*.

CHEETAH® train loves a song, zooming as it hums along.
It zooms across the land, past eggs, elephants and yellow sand.
Can you guess which sound is next?

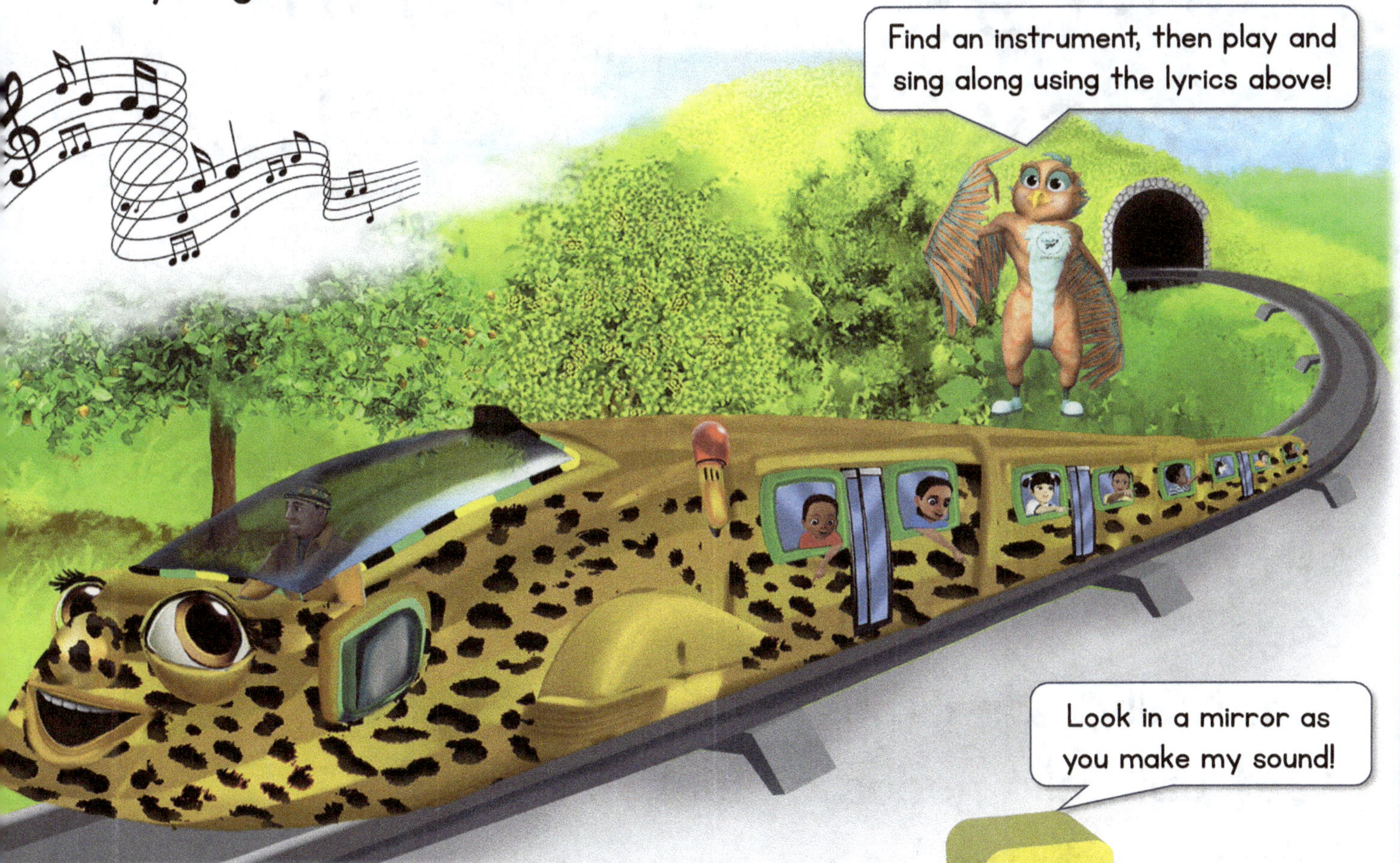
Find an instrument, then play and sing along using the lyrics above!

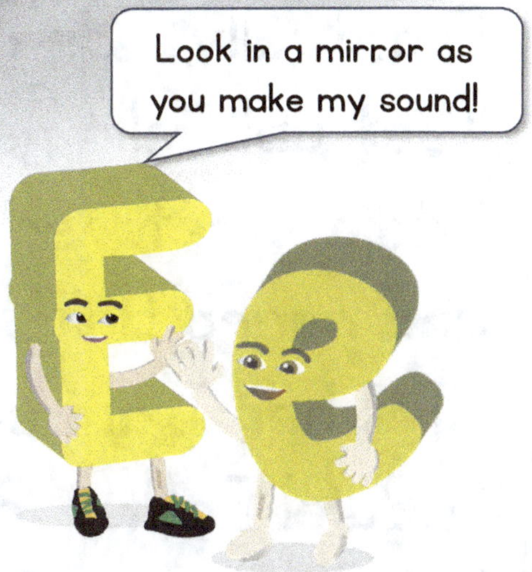
Look in a mirror as you make my sound!

The short ĕ sound is on the way to town.
The CHEETAH® train is slowing down.

Concept: phonic short ĕ

The **short ĕ** sound can appear at the start or in the middle of a word.

eggs

energy

every

red

hen

yellow

Eddie the Elephant

Every time Bella called to Eddie the elephant, he would run to her like a bullet train. "Eddie! Eddie!" Bella yelled one day. But Eddie was wearing earmuffs, sitting on the edge of a well, eating eggs.

Eventually, Edna the Hen tapped him with her elbow. "Get up! Bella needs a ride!" she said.

Eddie stretched his enormous ears and heard Bella yelling.

"Tell her I am eating," Eddie moaned.

"Eddie! Eddie!" Bella yelled. But Eddie, like everyone else, was very busy.

Apply: short ĕ

Listen to the word for each picture. Circle the picture if you hear the short ĕ sound.

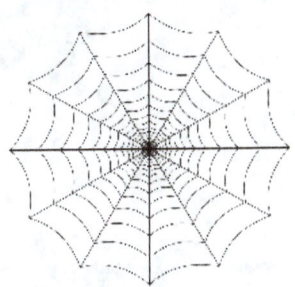   

Practise writing the letter e.

Smile a little and say ĕ sound. Keep your mouth small and relaxed.
Excellent!

Listen to the story. <u>Underline</u> the letter E or e if you hear the short ĕ sound.

Ted and Ben

At the end of the bend, Ted met Ben.

Then, they went to the den.

That is when Ted fed the red hen.

"Let us go to bed, it is very late," said Ted.

short ĕ sound = _____

My Word Wall

(from the story *Ben and the Hen*)

short Ĕ ĕ

| Ben | met | pet | hen |

| red | was | will |

| not | eat | my |

| every | egg |

Colour the words you know.
Do you give your best effort every day?

My Word Work Mats*

Say & tap · Map (sounds) · Graph (letters) · Check · Write it

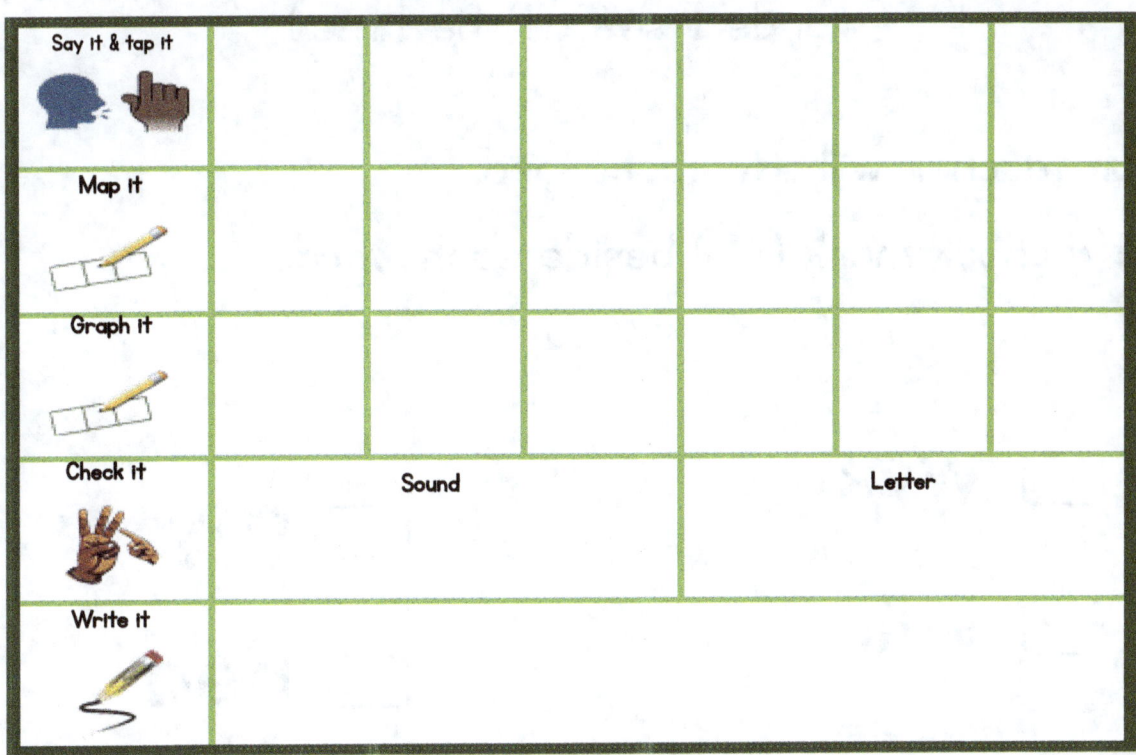

Say It & tap It					
Map It					
Graph It					
Check It	Sound			Letter	
Write It					

Say It & tap It				
Map It				
Graph It				
Check It	Sound		Letter	
Write It				

Put a ♥ above any part of the word that is tricky.

Get more words from C-DER® books 4, *Off to the Vet*, and 5, *Play Time with My Friends*. Use your poster to learn **-et** word families.

*Adapted and modified by CHEETAH® Toys & More, LLC for inclusion in this educational work.

Sight Words Activity

(words I see all the time)

Your teacher will say each word.

Put a check mark (✓) beside each word.

☐ **was**

☐ **will**

☐ **not**

☐ **eat**

☐ **my**

☐ **red**

☐ **every**

Sentences:

1. I am Ben.

2. The hen is red.

I can read with you!

Name: _____

Ben and the Hen

Ben met a pet hen.
The hen was red.
The hen ran to the pen.
The hen sat on an egg
in the pen.
Ben said, "I will not eat
my red hen."
Every hen is my pet.

Answer these questions:

1. Where did the hen go?

2. Why did Ben say he would not eat
the hen?

3. How is this story like something
that could happen on a farm or at
your home?

My Reading
Record

Reading #1: ____ WCPM
Reading #2: ____ WCPM
Reading #3: ____ WCPM

Practise: short ĕ

E is for exercise! Try out some different exercises and show them to your friends and family.

Reread the story *Ted and Ben.* Take turns reading while the *CHEETAH Reading Partner©* listens carefully.

It will help us check how many words you read correctly in one minute.

Remember to read your best; nice and smooth!

When you finish, the *CHEETAH Reading Partner©* will tell you how well you did. We will try again and see if you can read even better the next time!

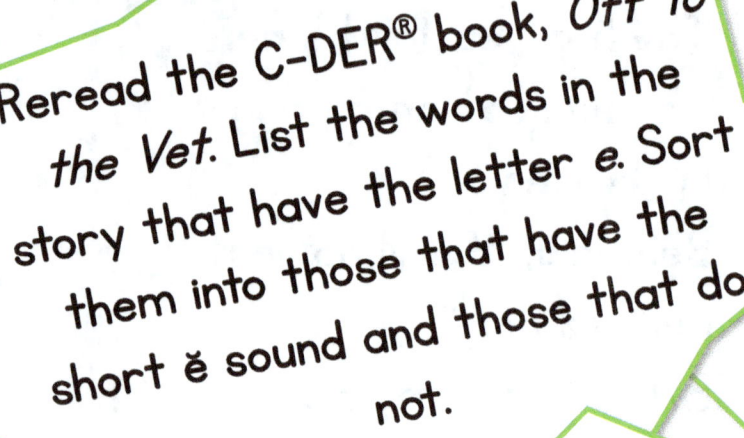

Reread the C-DER® book, *Off to the Vet.* List the words in the story that have the letter e. Sort them into those that have the short ĕ sound and those that do not.

Record yourself saying short ĕ words that rhyme.

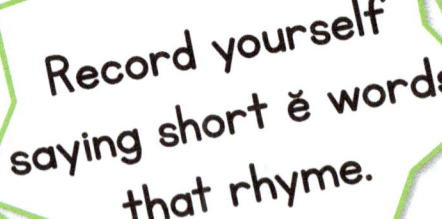

Pin letters on a line to make short ĕ words. Ask a friend to read them.

Use the CHEETAH® CVC puzzle pieces to make short ĕ words, such as "get".

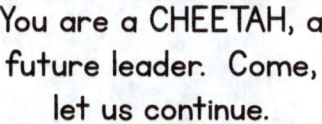
Evaluate: short ĕ

Colour the face that shows how you feel about the short ĕ sound.

Got it!

Almost got it

No, didn't get it

You are a CHEETAH, a future leader. Come, let us continue.

Dear Parent: Date: _____

_____ does/does not fully understand the phonic sound short ĕ. Please continue to review at home.

Signed: _____

Dear Teacher: Date: _____

Thank you. We have reviewed the phonic sound short ĕ together. My child had a chance to teach me.

Signed: _____

Reward sticker for parent or guardian goes here.

Well done!

Sticker for pupil goes here!

_____
(write name here)

understands the phonic sound short ĕ.

presents
House Flood
C-DER
presents
Fun with My Doll
C-DER

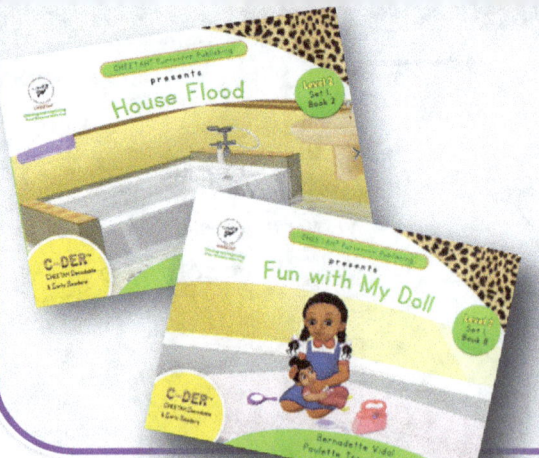

The /p/ sound

Let us read books 1, *At the Farm* (again); 6, *House Flood;* and 8, *Fun with My Doll.*

CHEETAH® train loves a song, zooming as it hums along.
It zooms beside the breeze, as pandas play in the trees.
Can you guess which sound is next?

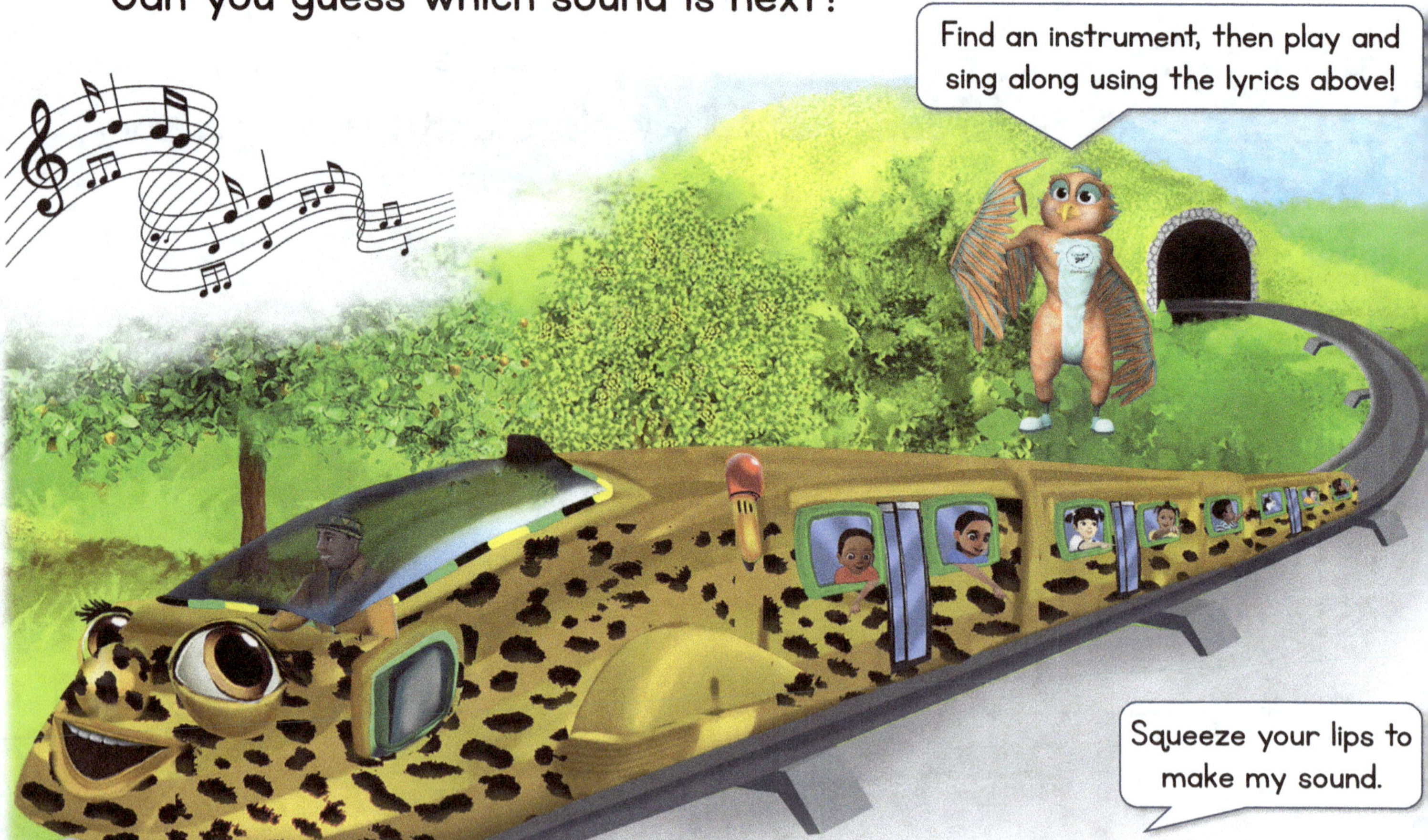
Find an instrument, then play and sing along using the lyrics above!
Squeeze your lips to make my sound.

The /p/ sound is on the way to town.
The CHEETAH® train is slowing down.

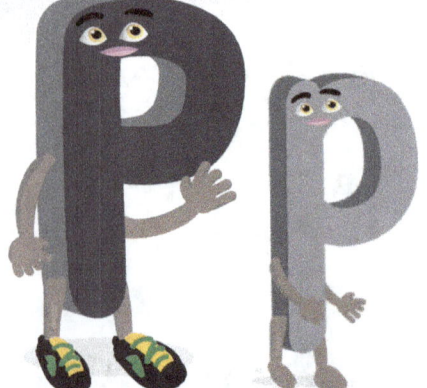

Concept: phonic sound /p/ 🔊

The /p/ sound can appear at the start, in the middle or at the end of a word. It can be made with one letter *p* or two letter *ps*.

pillow

put

pet

apple

happy

paper

ship

help

stop

Polly the Parrot 🔊

Pesky Polly was a pink parrot. She passed the time by playing 'Who am I?' with Sam. Pesky Polly always picked her favourite singer, Perfect Paula.

"You never pick any other person," moaned Sam.

"I will not pick Perfect Paula," said Pesky Polly. I promise to pick another pop star."

"Perfect!" said Sam.

Pesky Polly picked another person to be. Flap, flap, flap went her wings because she was very excited. Sam pulled Pesky Polly over to dance. "Let's party!"

74

Apply: /p/

Listen to the word for each picture. Draw a line from the picture to the big P if you hear the /p/ sound.

Practise writing the letter *p*.

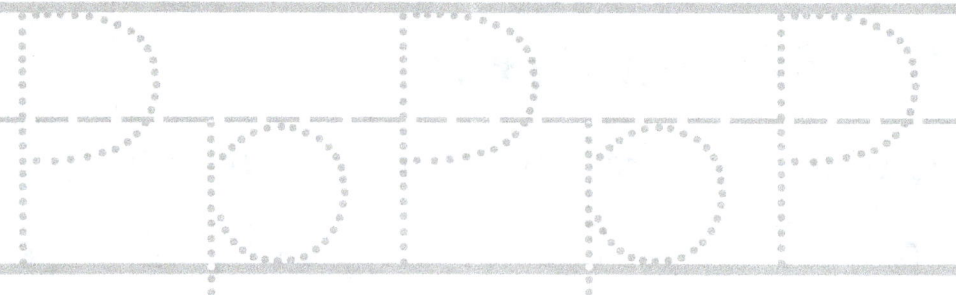

Press your lips, build up air, and pop.
Splendid!

Listen to the story. Circle the letter P or p if you hear the /p/ sound.

Pip's Pet Pig

Pip has a pink pet pig.

The pig loves to jump in the mud.

Pip says, "Pet pig! Get up, let us play!"

Pip and his pet have a super time.

/p/ sound = _____

P p

My Word Wall

(from the story *Pat and the Pig*)

pat	pig	pet	pip

pen	had	was

but	he	want	be

so	out	too

her	said	in

Colour the words you know.
You are a powerful pupil!

My Word Work Mats*

Say & tap · Map (sounds) · Graph (letters) · Check · Write it

P p

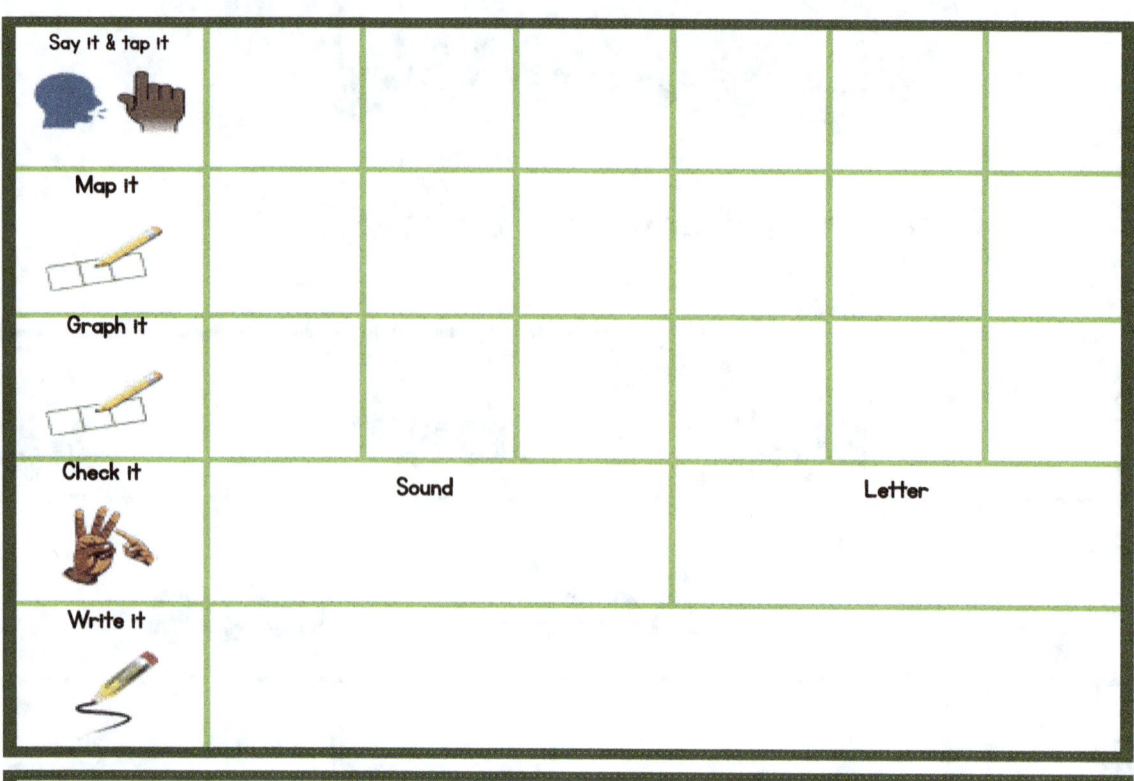

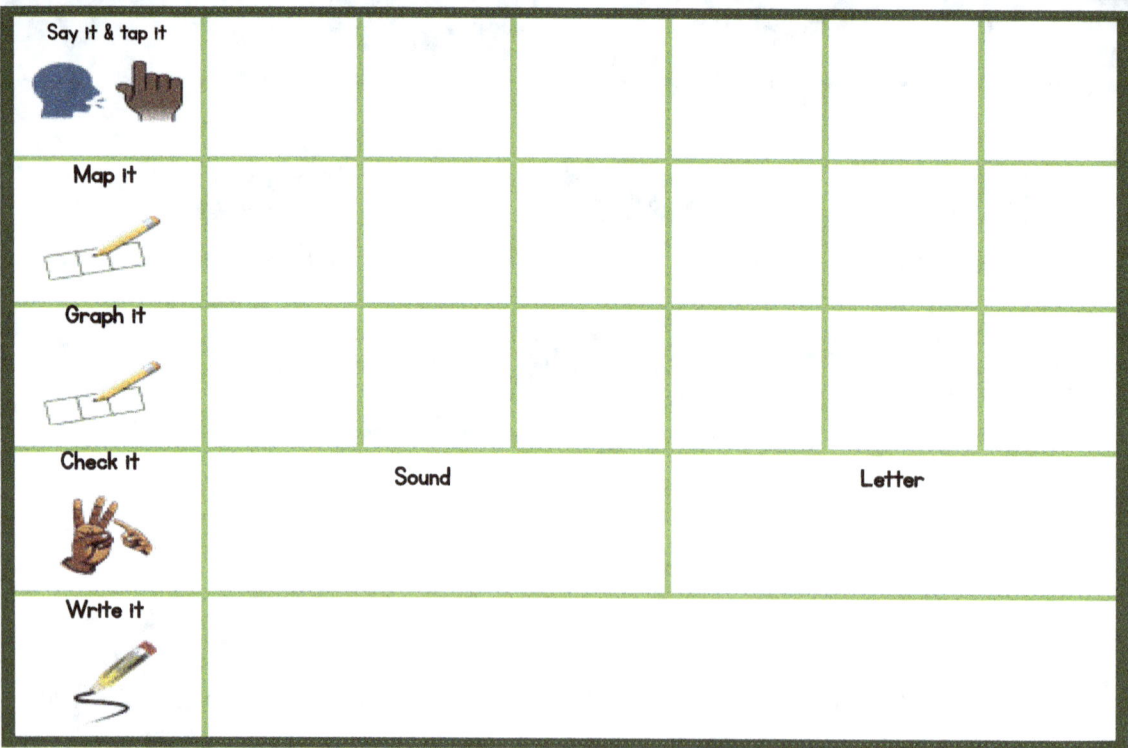

Put a 🧡 above any part of the word that is tricky.

Can you find five words with the **/p/** sound in C–DER® book 1, *At the Farm*? Read books 6, *House Flood*, and 8, *Fun with My Doll*. Use your poster to learn **-ip** words.

*Adapted and modified by CHEETAH® Toys & More, LLC for inclusion in this educational work.

Sight Words Activity

(words I see all the time)

Take turns doing a spelling test with a partner. One person says the word, and the other person writes it. Then switch!

was _____   so _____

in _____   out _____

but_____   too _____

he_____   her _____

want _____   said_____

be_____   in _____

Sentences:

1. Pat had a pig

2. Pip was in the pen.

I can read with you!

Name: _____

Pat and the Pig

Pat had a pet pig, Pip. Pip was in the pen, but he wanted to be in a pit. So, Pip ran out of the pen. Pat ran too. Pat did pat Pip, her pet pig. Pat said, "Pip, nap in the pen." Pip ran and sat in the pen. Pip the pig had a nap.

Answer these questions:

1. What problem did Pip cause for Pat?
2. How did Pat solve the problem?
3. Can you read the first sentence the way your teacher does?
4. What are the two meanings of Pat?
5. Why is Pat written with a capital letter?

My Reading Record

Reading #1: ____ WCPM
Reading #2: ____ WCPM
Reading #3: ____ WCPM

Practise: /p/

Make a post box by cutting a thin opening into a box that closes. Write words with the /p/ sound and post them.

Remove the words from the post box. Group the words according to whether the /p/ sound is at the beginning, middle or end.

Make a pig from a paper plate.

Reread the C-DER® book, *House Flood.* As part of a group, act out the events of the story, stating the action words that contain the /p/ sound.

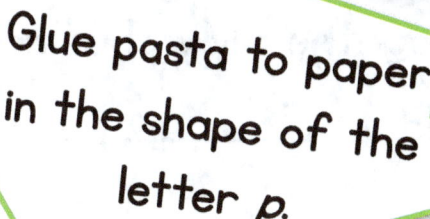

Glue pasta to paper in the shape of the letter *p*.

Say, "iCHEETAH©." Wait for it to say, "Cheetah to the rescue, how can I help you?" Then ask it to "create a story about a pig." Listen carefully, then talk about what happened first, next, and last. I will read the story again to see who was right.

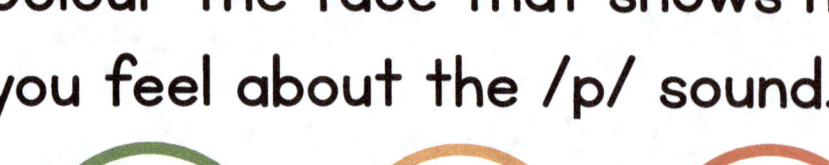

Evaluate: /p/

Colour the face that shows how you feel about the /p/ sound.

I believe in you. Let us take off together! Come wid mi!

Got it!   Almost got it   No, didn't get it

Dear Parent: Date: _____

_____ does/does not fully understand the phonic sound /p/. Please continue to review at home.

Signed: _____

Dear Teacher: Date: _____

Thank you. We have reviewed the phonic sound /p/ together. My child had a chance to teach me.

Signed: _____

Reward sticker for parent or guardian goes here.

Well done!

Sticker for pupil goes here!

_____
(write name here)

understands the phonic sound /p/.

CHEETAH® Review

Look at each row. (Circle) the picture that <u>starts</u> with the sound.

s	 saw	 man	 can
short a	 Pp	 ant	 monkey
m	 astronaut	 map	 hen
short e	 house	 bus	 elephant
p	 eggs	 pig	 saw

CHEETAH® Review

Use the letters to make as many short /a/ and /e/ words as you can. Letters can be used more than once. Be creative and have fun!

How many words did you make? Teach someone at home how to create words using letters.

CHEETAH® Review

Find the words below in the word search puzzle.

m	a	k	e	m
o	n	s	r	e
m	t	h	i	s
y	p	w	m	a
p	u	t	a	w

put   me   saw   this   make   my

How did you do? Did you learn anything
new? Come, let's go!
Learning never ends.

Solve the clues to complete the crossword.

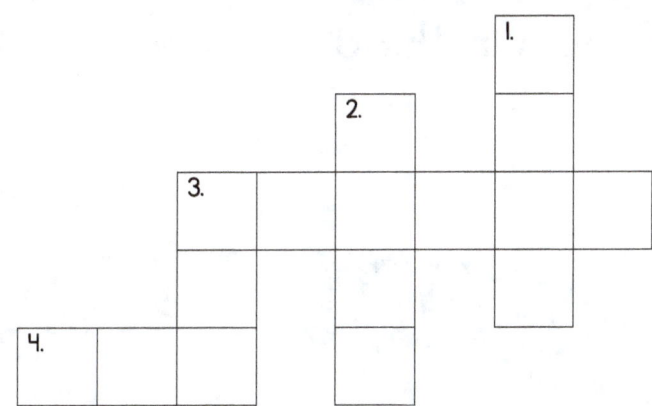

Across:

3. The colour of the sun.
4. The boy ___ red hair.

Down:

1. What cars do at a red traffic light.
2. This is what you do with your toys.
3. The word you say when you agree.

Let's create words

Complete the table. Put the letters together to make words.

Beginning sound	Middle sound	Ending sound	Words created
s	a	t	sat, set, mat, met, pat, pet
m		m	
p	e	p	

List the words that you do not know the meaning of.

_____

_____

Ask an adult what they mean.

Sound out the words you have made.

Let's put together

Connect the boxes to make words from the –am word family. Write them in the given space.

p

t   -am

m

pam

_____

_____

_____

Words in a word family all share the same sound.

Let's take apart

Break each word into sounds. Write the letters that make each sound.

A unit of sound is a phoneme.

Let's trace

Trace the letters to write sentences.

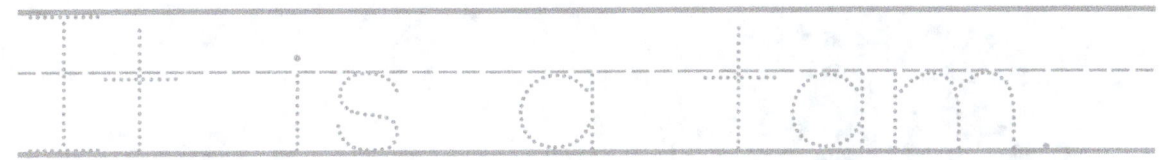

Read the sentences you have written.

I know you have some superpowers that are also called magical powers! You can work on some of your powers for them to become superpowers. Practise, practise, practise. Is hearing one of your powers? Can you hear the unique sound that each letter makes? Can you put the sounds of letters together to make words? Can you read? Your magical powers of hearing will also help to get the superpower of reading!

CHEETAH® Reward Stickers

Did you have fun? I did!

88

This page has been left blank so you can cut out the reward stickers.

Please refer to the corresponding CHEETAH® Poster Stories© and fluency tests for this set's focus sounds. Additionally, the following C-DER® books are recommended for comprehension and fluency practise:

Sound	C-DER® reference	Book title
f	Set 2, book 9	My Brother Jim
n	Set 2, book 10	Guess What?
short ĭ	Set 2, book 12	A Day in My Life
t	Set 1, book 4	Off to the Vet
r	Set 2, book 15	Come Back, Tam!

Teaching tips*:

- The /f/ sound is made by pressing the front teeth to the lower lip and breathing through the opening.
- The /n/ sound is made through the nose. Press your tongue against the roof of your mouth and engage your vocal cords.
- The short ĭ sound is pronounced 'ih' as in 'pig'.
- Make sure the /t/ sound is not pronounced 'tuh' – leave off the 'uh.'
- Make sure the /r/ sound is pronounced /rrrrrrrr/, not 'ruh.'

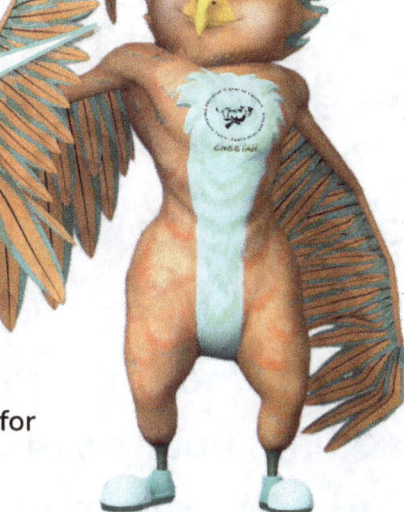

Come wid mi. Mek wi soar to a new reading level. Together we

*Please see the appendices and the Pupil Helper's book for additional tips.

 # Did You Know? #1

For Most Students Daily Reading Builds Vocabulary Fast

Daily Reading Minutes → Words Seen Per Year

(Anderson, Wilson & Fielding, 1988)

5 minutes/day → about 282,000 words a year

10 minutes/day → about 622,000 words a year

20 minutes/day → ebout 1,8 million words a year

More than 20 minutes/day – exposure grows even faster and the vocabulary gap widen sharply

Children who see more words each day develop stronger decoding, fluency, and comprehension skills - the foundations of reading success.

Let us read book 9,
My Brother Jim.

CHEETAH® train loves a song, zooming as it hums along.
Funny noises came from the sea. Flying fish are flipping free!
Can you guess which sound is next?

Find an instrument, then play and sing along using the lyrics above!

Where do you place your tongue when you make my sound?

The /f/ sound is on the way to town.
The CHEETAH® train is slowing down.

Concept: phonic sound /f/

The /f/ sound can appear at the start, in the middle or at the end of a word.

Ff

fan

find

fin

so**f**a

o**ff**ice

break**f**ast

lea**f**

roo**f**

cli**ff**

Feri the Fox

Feri the fox loved to have fun. At four o'clock, he grabbed his stuff and went to find Fay at the farm. "Hi Feri," said Fay. "I can play in five minutes." Feri the fox waited on the fence and fanned his face.

Farmer Finn was feeling tired. Farmer Finn sat on the fence and heard a funny sound. Oh no! Fay ran over as fast as she could. "You are sitting on my Feri the fox!" Fay told the farmer. As fast as he could, farmer Finn jumped up off the fence.

"I am fine!" laughed Feri the fox, and they all went to have fun.

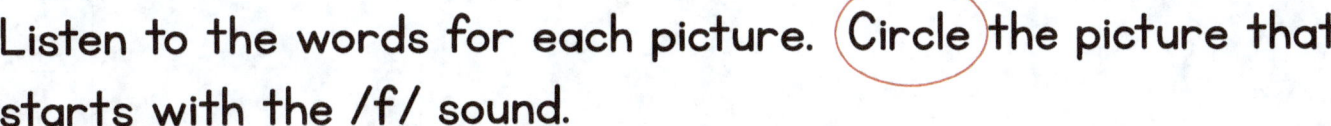
Listen to the words for each picture. (Circle) the picture that starts with the /f/ sound.

 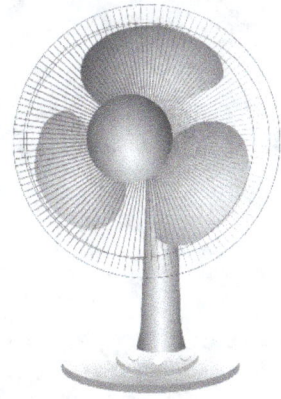 

Practise writing the letter *f*.

Bite your bottom lip softly and blow air out.
Fantastic!

Listen to the story. (Circle) the letter F or f if you hear the  /f/ sound.

Fun with Feri

Feri the fox sat on a leaf.

"I can leap far," he said.

"No fox can fly, but all foxes can jump!"

Feri was full of fun.

/f/ sound = _____

Ff

My Word Wall

(from the story Fin and the Fan)

Fin	fit	fan	fun
	on	with	my
	have	the	sit

Colour the words you know.
You are fantastic and fearless!

My Word Work Mats*

Say & tap · Map (sounds) · Graph (letters) · Check · Write it

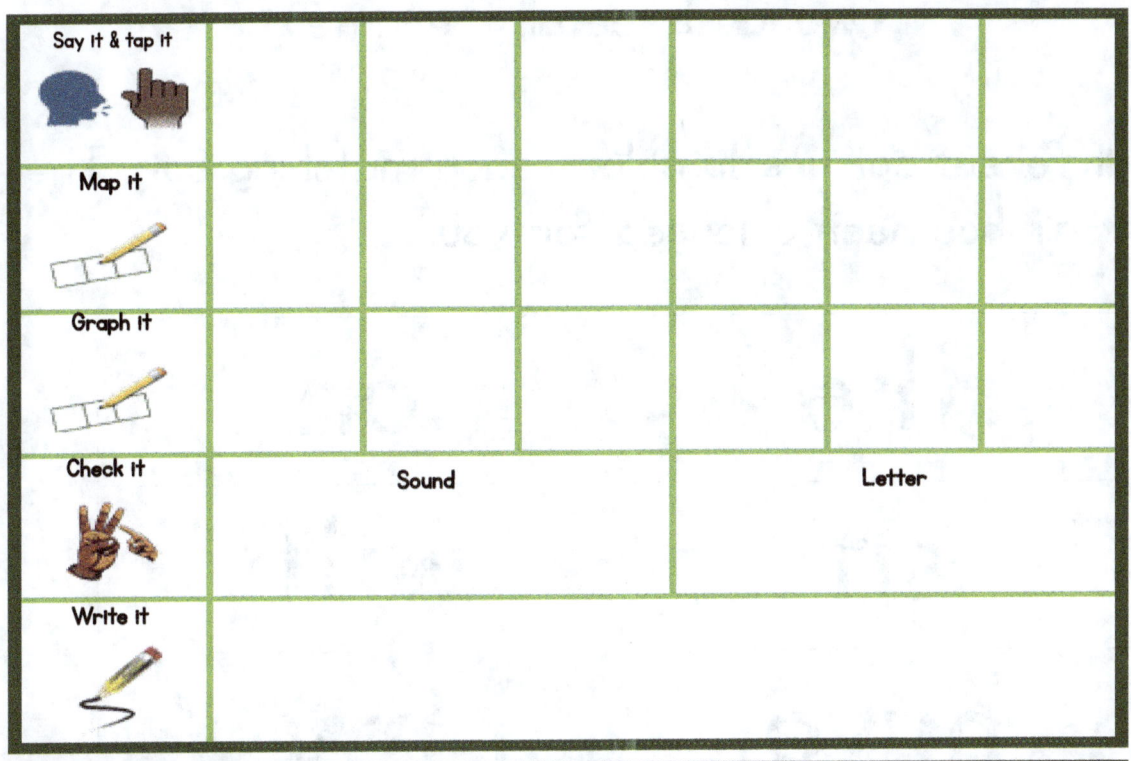

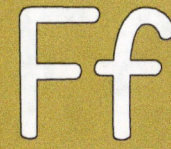

Ff

Say it & tap it						
Map it						
Graph it						
Check it	Sound			Letter		
Write it						

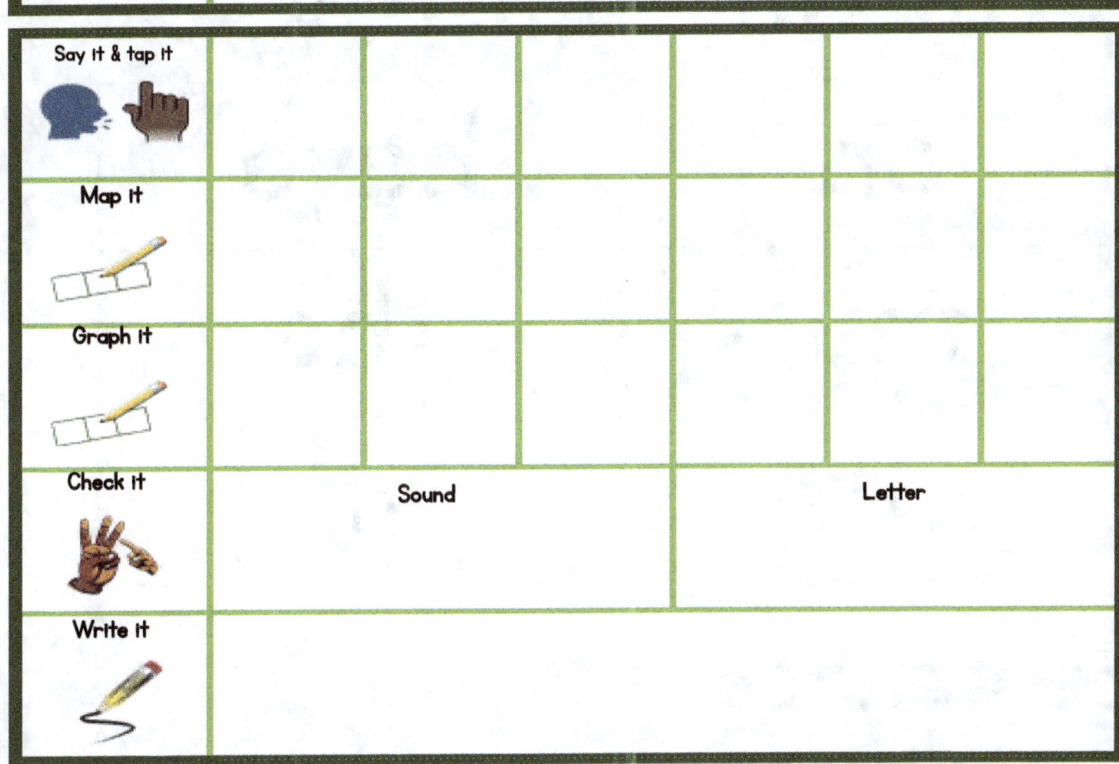

Say it & tap it						
Map it						
Graph it						
Check it	Sound			Letter		
Write it						

Put a ♥ above any part of the word that is tricky.

Read C-DER® book 9, *My Brother Jim*. Use your poster to learn -it word families!

*Adapted and modified by CHEETAH® Toys & More, LLC for inclusion in this educational work.

Sight Words Activity

(words I see all the time)

Use different colours to colour each matching pair. The first pair has been coloured for you.

the	on
sit	with
have	my
on	have
my	the
with	sit

Sentences:

1. I am Tim.

2. I sit on a mat.

I can read with you!

Ff

Name: _____

Fin and the Fan

I am Fin.

I am fit.

I sit on a mat with my fan.

I have fun on the mat.

Answer these questions:

1. Who sat on the mat?

2. Why do you think Fin had fun on the mat?

3. What did Fin have with him?

My Reading Record

Reading #1: _____ WCPM
Reading #2: _____ WCPM
Reading #3: _____ WCPM

98

Practise: /f/

Ask iCHEETAH© to create a short story about a fish.

Listen carefully, and at the end of the story, tell me one thing the fish did .

Use your fingers to finger paint things that begin with the letter f.

Watch videos of frogs on the internet. Draw a frog and tell the class about your frog. Do any other animal names begin with the letter f?

Paint a leaf. Use the painted leaf to make patterns on a blank page.

Reread the C-DER® book, My Brother Jim. List the words with the /f/ sound. How many f words did you find?

F is for fabric. Draw an outline of the letter f then cut and stick pieces of fabric inside the letter.

Colour the face that shows how you feel about the /f/ sound.

Got it!   **Almost got it**   **No, didn't get it**

Keep flying high with your learning. The sky is the limit! Come wid me!

Dear Parent: Date: _____

_____ does/does not fully understand the phonic sound /f/. Please continue to review at home.

Signed: _____

Dear Teacher: Date: _____

Thank you. We have reviewed the phonic sound /f/ together. My child had a chance to teach me.

Signed: _____

Reward sticker for parent or guardian goes here.

Well done!

_____
(write name here)

understands the phonic sound /f/.

Sticker for pupil goes here!

Let us read book 10,
Guess What?

CHEETAH® train loves a song, zooming as it hums along.
An ant is on Sam's neck. Its nest is nowhere on the deck!
Can you guess which sound is next?

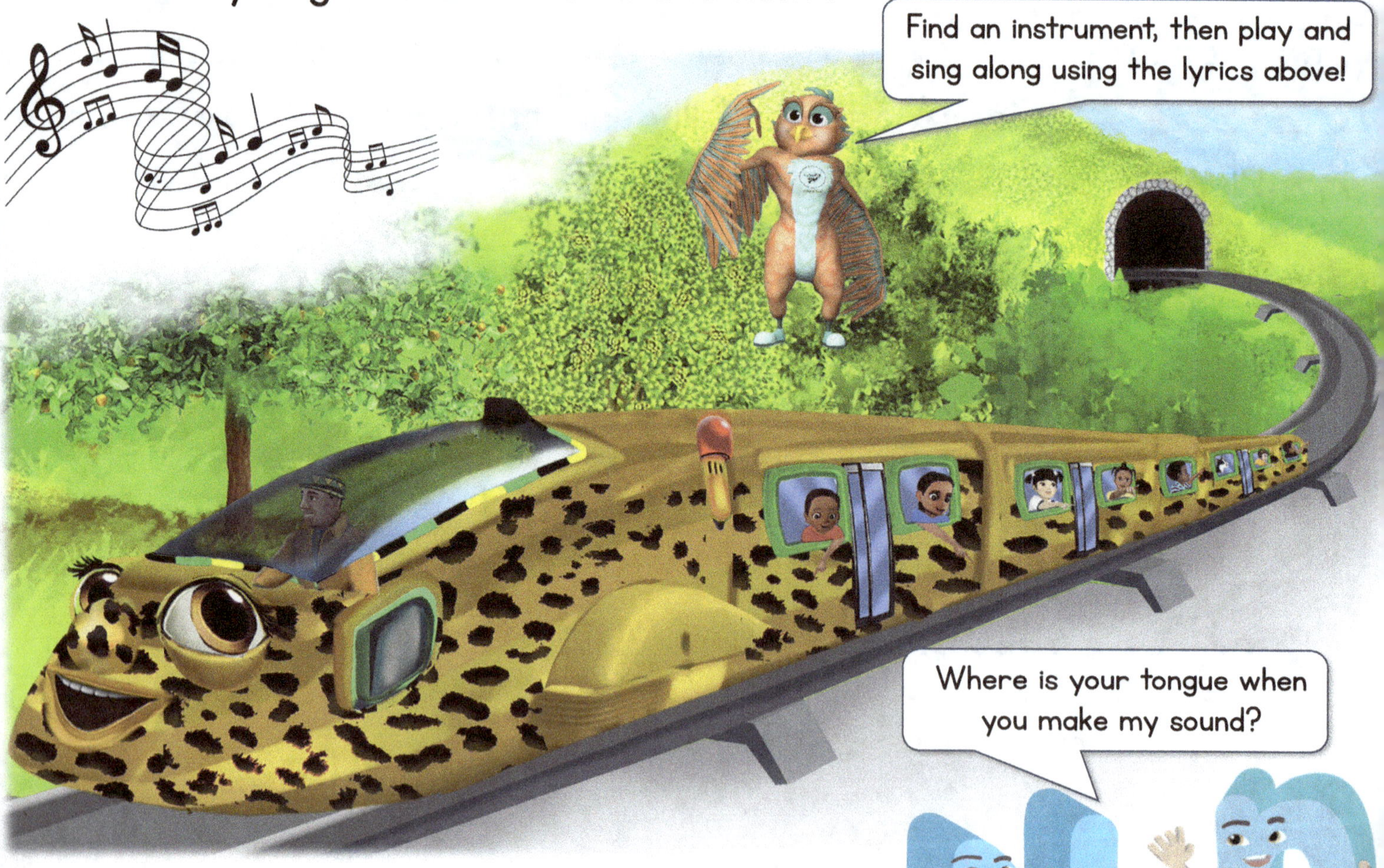

Find an instrument, then play and sing along using the lyrics above!

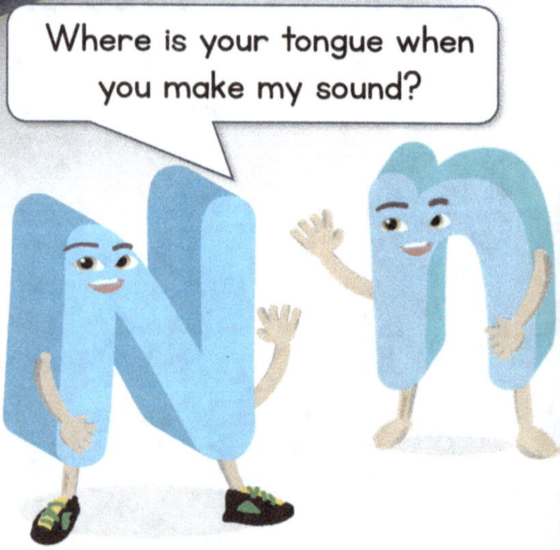

Where is your tongue when you make my sound?

The /n/ sound is on the way to town.
The CHEETAH® train is slowing down.

Concept: phonic sound /n/ 🔊

The /n/ sound can appear at the start, in the middle or at the end of a word.

Nn

nurse   **tunnel**   **brown**

not   **into**   **down**

now   **money**   **soon**

Ned Had a Nap 🔊

Ned had a nap. He dreamt he was racing a green car. It was very fast. He had the number nine on the back. Soon, he had raced past ten cars. Ned noticed there were no more cars ahead of him. Ned had won the race!

"I have never won a race before now!" said Ned. But then he woke up under a tree.

"Oh no, it was only a dream and not a real race," he said. Ned was not happy. But when Ned looked down,

he saw a shining medal around his neck.

"It is true!" said Ned. "I can win races after all!"

Apply: /n/

Say the words of each picture. Circle all the pictures that have the /n/ sound.

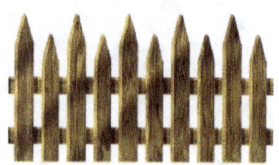

Practise writing the letter *n*.

> Touch your tongue behind your top teeth and hum through your nose.
>
> Excellent!

Listen to the story. Circle the letter N or n if you hear the /n/ sound.

Ned at Night

I am Ned. I nod when I am tired.

At nap time, I snore and snore.

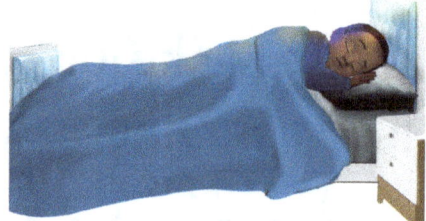

When night comes, it is easy to find me.

I am nicely tucked into my neat bed!

/n/ sound = _____

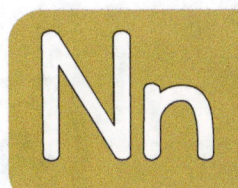

Nn

My Word Wall

(from the story Ned and the Net)

Ned	nine	net	nip
now	saw	were	
was	them	said	

Colour the words you know.
Never give up!

104

My Word Work Mats*

Say & tap · Map (sounds) · Graph (letters) · Check · Write it

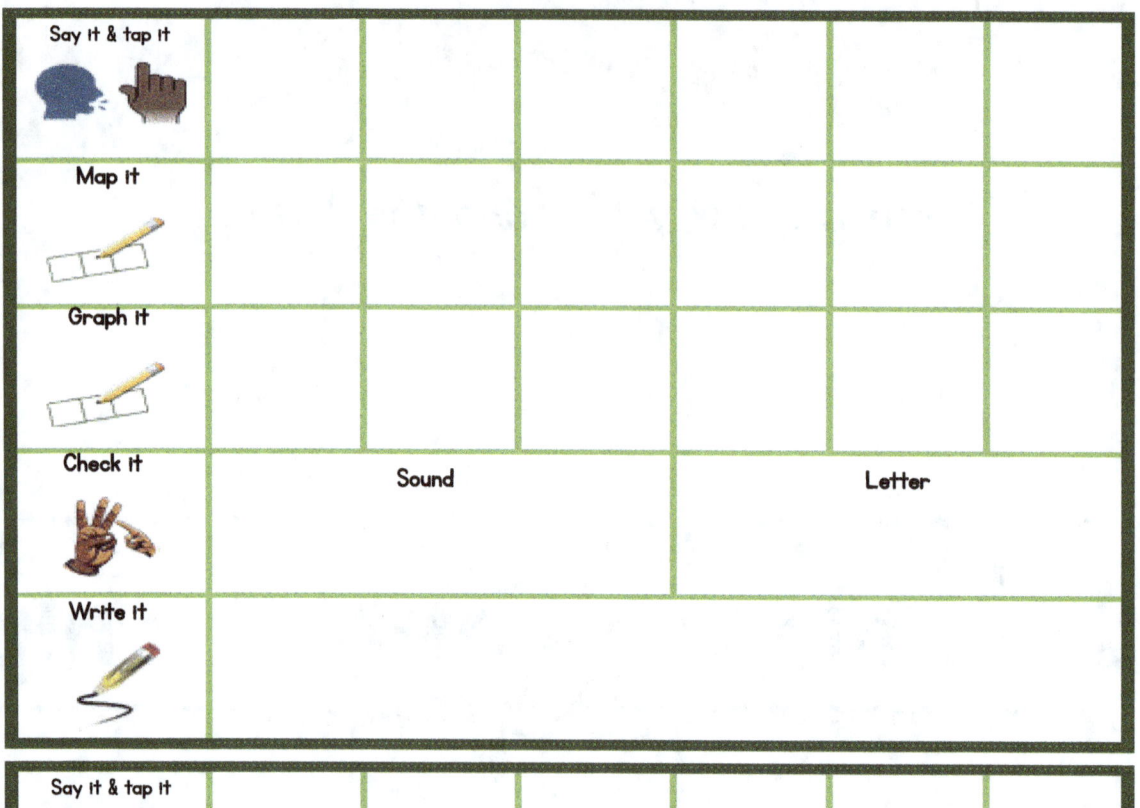

Learn more words from C-DER® book 10, *Guess What.* Use your poster to learn **-in** word families!

Put a 💚 above any part of the word that is tricky.

*Adapted and modified by CHEETAH® Toys & More, LLC for inclusion in this educational work.

105

Sight Words Activity

(words I see all the time)

Draw a line to find the matching words. One is already done for you.

Column A	Column B
ran	could
saw	them
were	said
was	did
them	not
said	help
did	it
not	saw
it	were
could	was
help	ran

Sentences:

1. Ned saw the rats.

2. The rats ran.

I can read with you!

Name: _____

Ned and the Net

By Paul Law

Ned saw nine rats .
The rats were in a big net.
Ned was sad for them.
Ned said, "Rats, nip the net.
Nip it now!"
The rats sat but did not
nip the net.
Could Ned help?

Answer these questions:

1. What problem did the rats have?

2. Based on the picture, how could Ned help the rats?

3. What is the name of this story?

4. Who is the author of the story?

My Reading Record

Reading #1: ____ WCPM
Reading #2: ____ WCPM
Reading #3: ____ WCPM

Practise: /n/

Choose 6 CHEETAH® sight words cards that contain the /n/ sound. Number them 1-6. Roll a die and read the word with that number.

Reread the *C-DER®* book, *Guess What?* Look for 2-letter *n* words and use the CHEETAH® letters to recreate them. Repeat for 3- and 4-letter /n/ words.

Play the *Guess What?* game for /n/ sound words with a group of friends.

Use the CHEETAH® Reading Partner© to read *Ben and the Hen*. Take turns reading while the CHEETAH® Reading Partner listens. It will tell you how well you read and cheer you on when you finish.

N is for numbers! Make the numbers 1-10. Which of the numbers have the /n/ sound in their name?

Use the CHEETAH® Reading Partner ChatGPT link to get pupils reading levels.

Colour the face that shows how you feel about the /n/ sound.

Got it!

Almost got it

No, didn't get it

Ready for take-off? Let us find out what the next sound is! Come wid mi!

Dear Parent: Date: _____

_____ does/does not fully understand the phonic sound /n/. Please continue to review at home.

Signed: _____

Dear Teacher: Date: _____

Thank you. We have reviewed the phonic sound /n/ together. My child had a chance to teach me.

Signed: _____

Reward sticker for parent or guardian goes here.

Well done!

Sticker for pupil goes here!

_____
(write name here)

understands the phonic sound /n/.

Let us read book 12,
A Day in My Life

CHEETAH® train plays a song, zooming as it hums along.
Over there a silly pig is itching in a frilly wig.
Can you guess which sound is next?

Find an instrument, then play and sing along using the lyrics above!

Can you make my sound 3 times?

The short ĭ sound is on the way to town.
The CHEETAH® train is slowing down.

Concept: phonic sound short ĭ

The short ĭ sound can appear at the start or in the middle of a word.

i

insect

is

it

ship

big

little

Jim and Jill

Jim and Jill were twins. Their uncle Bill had a ship. He would lick his lips and tell them tales of his adventures.

One day, he told them about a big magic pig with fins and gills, swimming in the sea. It bit his ship and water spilled in. Soon the ship began to sink.

"I had to be quick to save my ship!" he said. "So, I put the tip of a thick stick inside the hole, until the ship got back to the docks."

"Is that a true story?" asked Jim.

Uncle Bill winked and poured the twins a glass of milk.

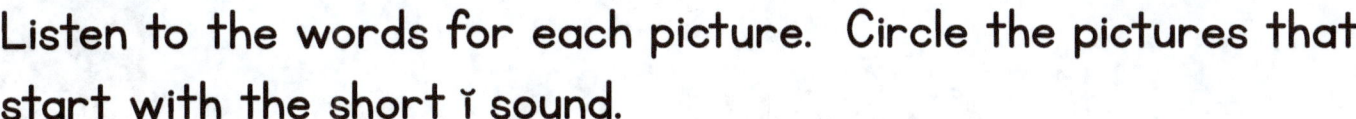

Apply: short ĭ

Listen to the words for each picture. Circle the pictures that start with the short ĭ sound.

Practise writing the letter *i*.

Smile and say ĭ ĭ like in itch – keep your mouth small.

Keep it up!

Listen to the story. <u>Underline</u> the letter I or i if you hear the short ĭ sound.

Fish for Jim

Jim got a gift. It was two fish.

He put the fish in a jar to swim.

"Big fish, little fish," said Jim.

"Swim, swim, swim and make a wish."

short ĭ sound = _____

My Word Wall

(from the story *Fin in the Tin*)

insect	in	it	into

please	go	away

said	his	did	sit

Colour the words you know.
Never give up!

My Word Work Mats*

Say & tap · Map (sounds) · Graph (letters) · Check · Write it

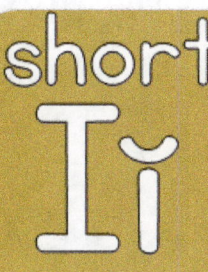

short
I i

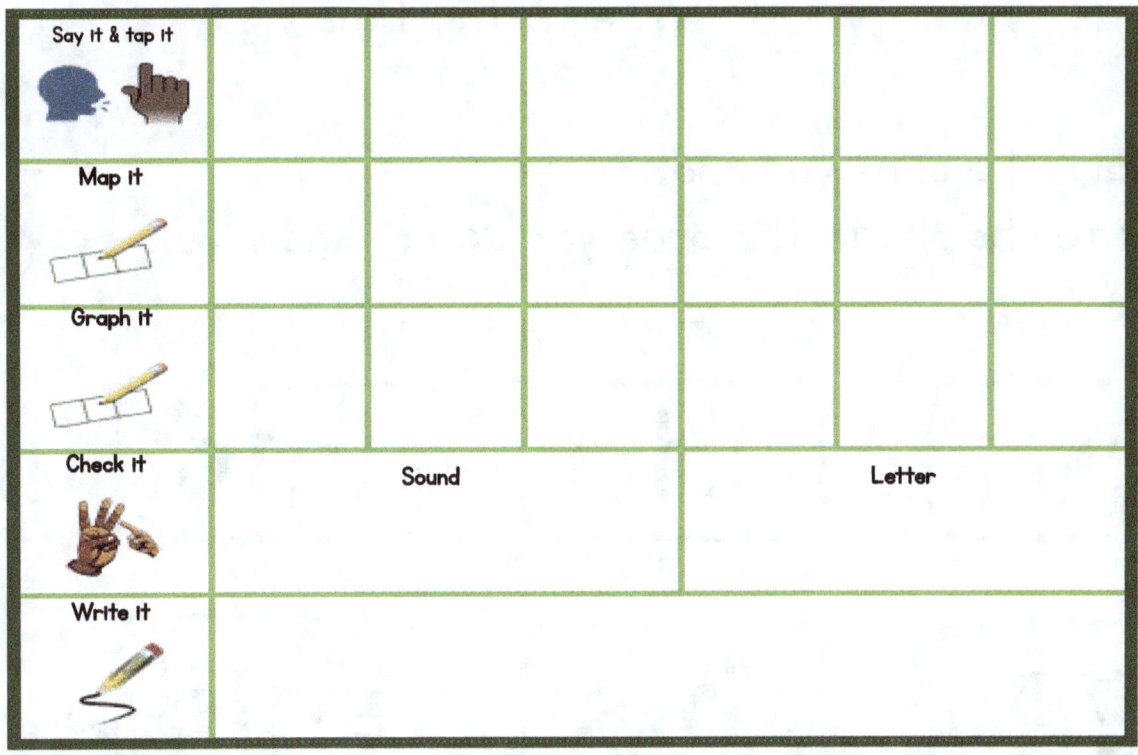

Say It & tap It					
Map It					
Graph It					
Check It	Sound			Letter	
Write It					

Say It & tap It					
Map It					
Graph It					
Check It	Sound			Letter	
Write It					

Put a ❤ above any part of the word that is tricky.

Get more words from C-DER® book 12, *A Day in My Life.* Use your poster to learn more **-it** word families.

*Adapted and modified by CHEETAH® Toys & More, LLC for inclusion in this educational work.

Sight Words Activity

(words I see all the time)

Colour the ones you know.
Ask for help with the ones you do not know yet.

in	it	into
go	his	said
did	please	away

Sentences:

1. Tin is in a tin.
2. The insect ran.
3. Tin did nap.

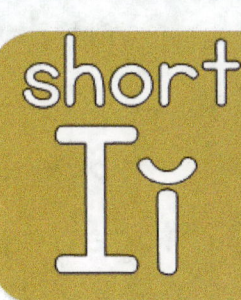

I can read with you!

Name: _____

Fin in the Tin

Fin is in a big tin.
Fin did sit in it.
A big insect bit the tin.
It ran into the tin.
Fin hid.
"Please go away," Fin said.
The big insect cannot fit in the tin.
So, the insect ran.
Fin sat in the tin.
Fin did nap in his big tin.

Answer these questions:

1. Where was Fin during most of the story?
   A. in a tin
   B. on a mat

2. The insect _____.
   A. bit the tin
   B. sat on Fin

My Reading Record

Reading #1: ____ WCPM
Reading #2: ____ WCPM
Reading #3: ____ WCPM

3. Why did Fin hide?
   A. He saw the insect.
   B. He was cold.

Practise: short ĭ

Glue icicle sticks together to make the capital letter i, then paint it pink.

Use the CHEETAH® CVC puzzle pieces to make short ĭ words.

Reread the *C-DER®* book, *A Day in My Life*. Sort the short i words into those in the 'it' family and those not in the 'it' family.

I is for insects. Head outside and see how many different insects you can find. Take photographs of them. Use craft materials to make models of the insects you saw.

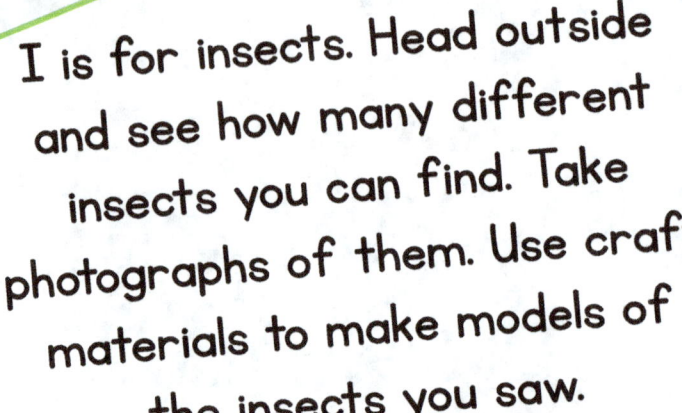

Make an igloo from building blocks.

Have a friend hide sight words cards around the room. You have 5 minutes to find as many short ĭ words as you can!

Ask iCHEETAH© to explain the different types of fish found in the sea.

JamDER⁺
Jamaican Decodable & Early Readers

Evaluate: short ĭ

Colour the face that shows how you feel about the short ĭ sound.

Got it!

Almost got it

No, didn't get it

You are learning more and more every day. Keep aiming for the sky! Come wid mi!

Dear Parent: Date: _____

_____ does/does not fully understand the phonic sound short ĭ. Please continue to review at home.

Signed: _____

Dear Teacher: Date: _____

Thank you. We have reviewed the phonic sound short ĭ together. My child had a chance to teach me.

Signed: _____

Reward sticker for parent or guardian goes here.

Well done!

_____
(write name here)

Sticker for pupil goes here!

understands the phonic sound short ĭ.

Let us read book 4,
Off to the Vet

CHEETAH® train loves a song, zooming as it hums along.
Terry loves to eat! Tomatoes are her favourite treat.
Can you guess which sound is next?

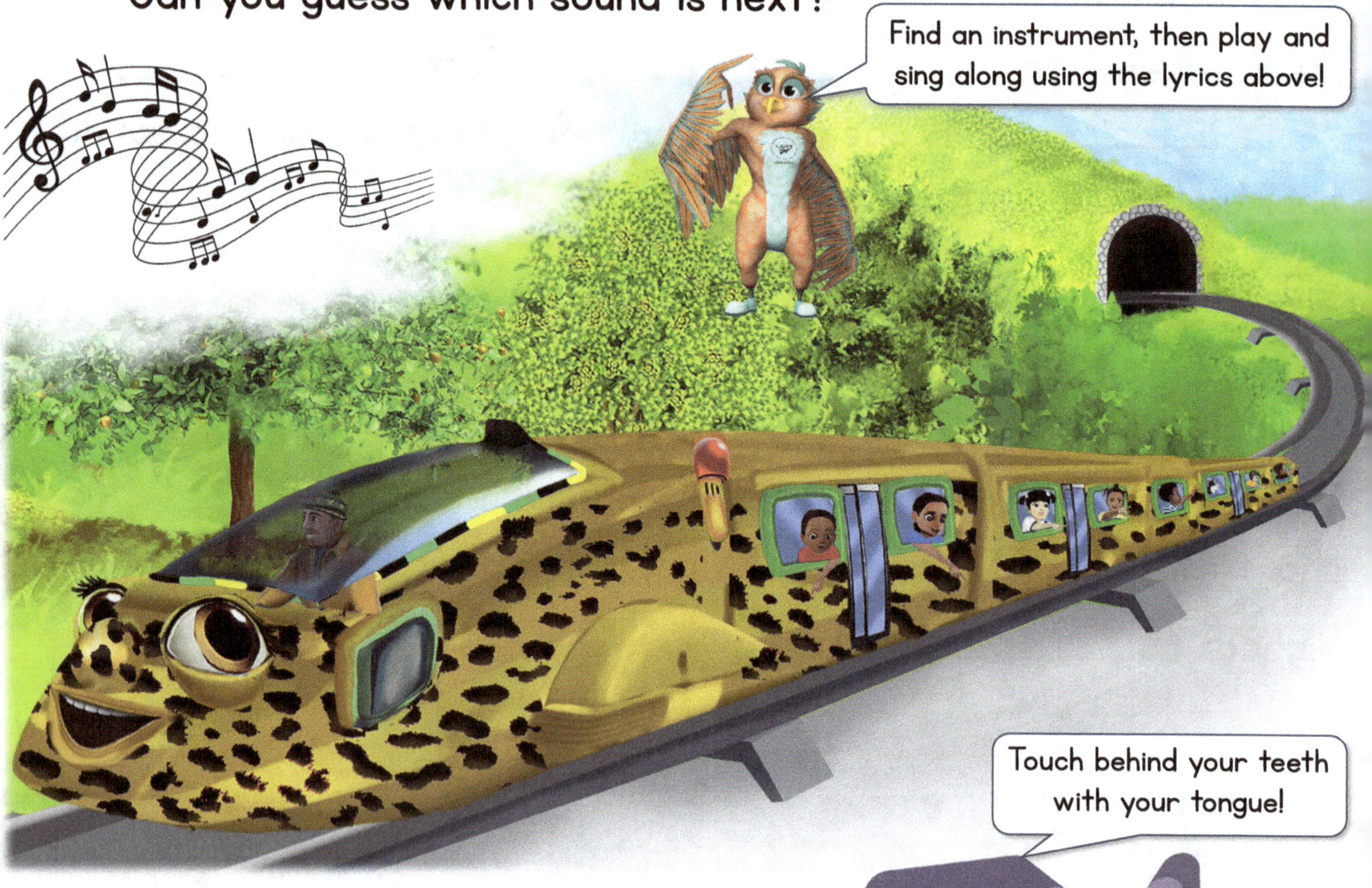

Find an instrument, then play and sing along using the lyrics above!

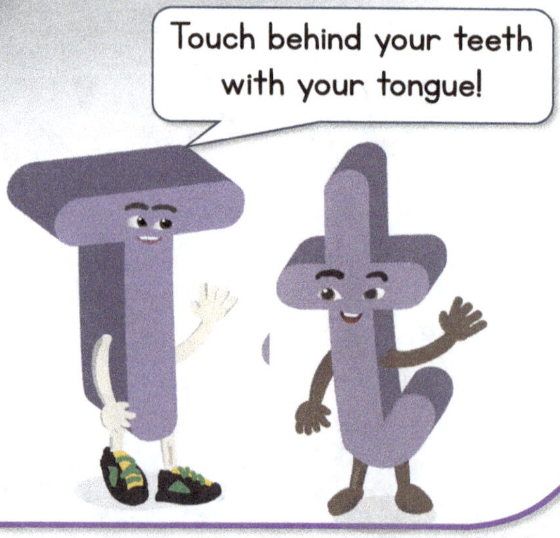

Touch behind your teeth with your tongue!

The /t/ sound is on the way to town.
The CHEETAH® train is slowing down.

Concept: phonic sound /t/

The /t/ sound can appear at the start, in the middle or at the end of a word.

toy	letter	cat
two	actor	not
take	pretty	but

Terry and Tomatoes

Terry the teddy bear loved to eat tomatoes.
She would squash them and drink the juice too.
Tiger Tim told her she would turn into a tomato
if she kept eating them.
"I will only eat two more!" cried Terry as
she ate them up.
"But look at your face," said Tiger Tim,
twirling his tail. "It is starting to turn red!"
Terry looked into a mirror. Her face was not red at all.
She heard Tim laugh.

"I was only joking," said Tim. "But tomato juice is on
your shirt. Time to take it off and wash it."

Apply: /t/ sound

Say the name of each animal. Draw lines to guide the ones with the /t/ sound to the tent.

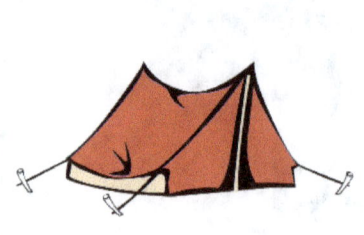

Practise writing the letter *t.*

Tap your tongue behind your top teeth and let go quickly.

Terrific!

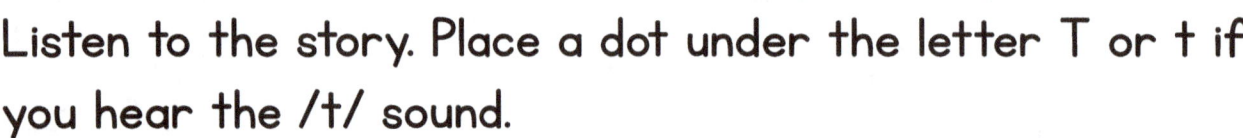

Listen to the story. Place a dot under the letter T or t if you hear the /t/ sound.

Tom Tiny Toy

Tom has a tiny toy tiger.

He takes it to school every day.

The toy tiger sits on his table.

Tom and his tiger like to tell tales.

/t/ sound = _____

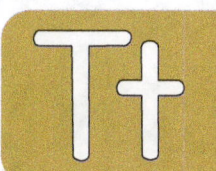

My Word Wall

(from the story *Tam and the Tin Set*)

Tam	tin	ten	tap
	tip	set	pit
the	was	in	could
	she	had	

Colour the words you know.
You read, you try, you triumph!

My Word Work Mats*

Say & tap · Map (sounds) · Graph (letters) · Check · Write it

T†

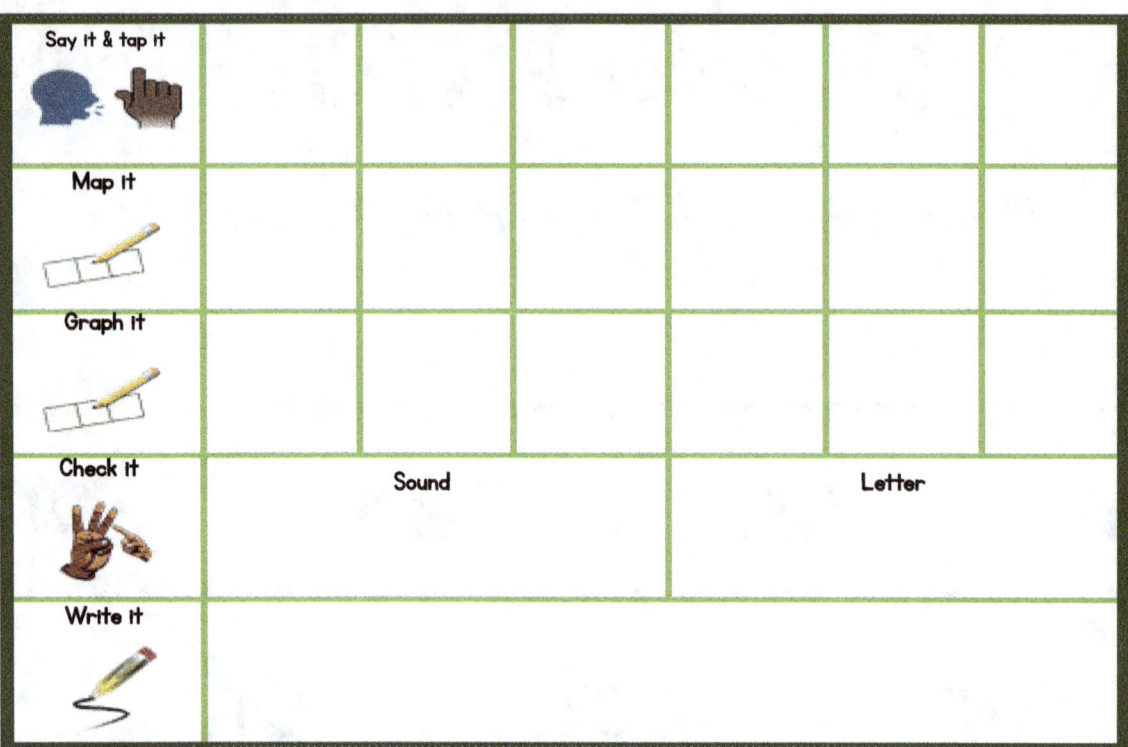

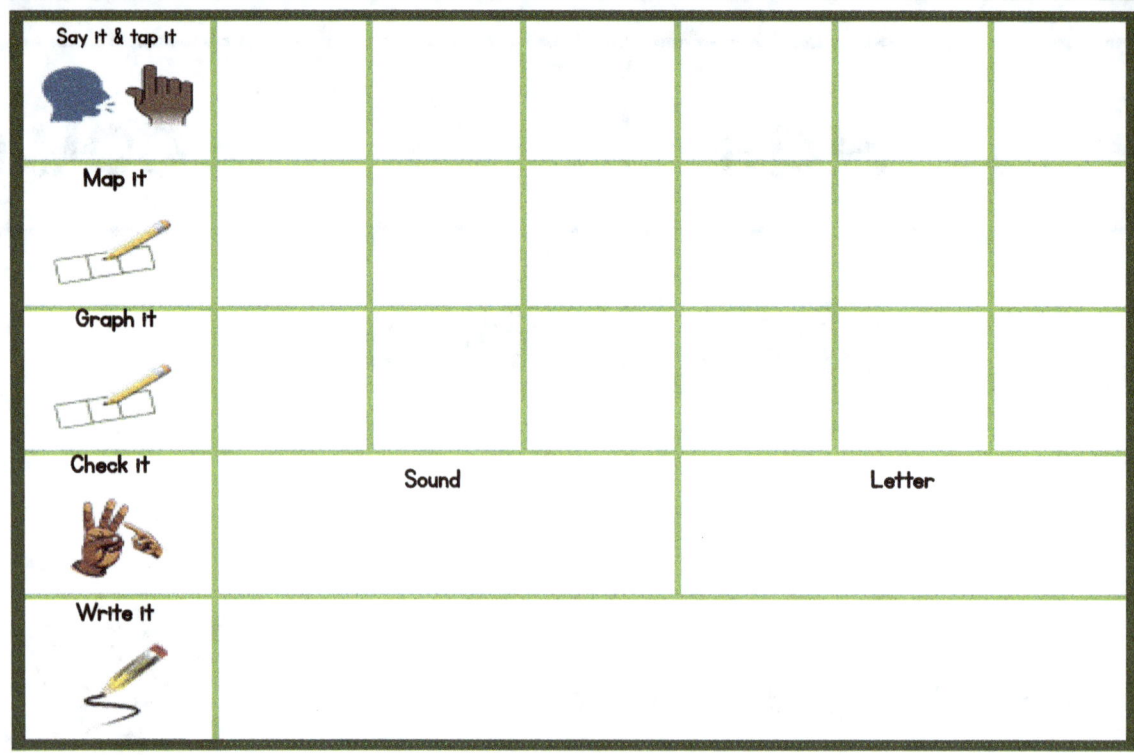

Put a ♥ above any part of the word that is tricky.

Get more words from C–DER® book 4, *Off to the Vet.* Use your poster to learn **-en** words.

*Adapted and modified by CHEETAH® Toys & More, LLC for inclusion in this educational work.

Sight Words Activity

(words I see all the time)

Trace each word, then say it out loud.

the   was

she   could

in   had

Sentences:

1. I am sat on a mat.
2. She had a tin.

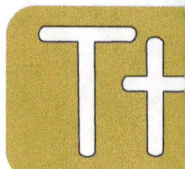

I can read with you!

Name: _____

T t

Tam and the Tin Set

Tam sat on a mat.
She had a tin set.
The tin set was in the pit.
Tam gave ten taps on the tin set.
Tap, tap, tap, tap!
Tap, tap, tap, tap!
Tap, tap!
Could Tam get a tip?

Answer these questions:

1. What did Tam have on the mat?

2. What did she do with her tin set?

3. How would you feel if you could play a tin set like Tam?

My Reading Record

Reading #1: _____ WCPM
Reading #2: _____ WCPM
Reading #3: _____ WCPM

Practise: /t/

What do you think "vet" means? Tell your partner. Now, use *iCHEETAH©* to check.

As part of a group, make a tree display. Cut out breadfruit shapes and write *t* words inside. Add them to the tree.

Make a turtle from a paper plate. Write the letter *t* on its shell.

Together we will reread the *C-DER®* book, *Off to the Vet*. Whenever you hear a word with the /t/ sound, stand up and make the shape of the letter *t*.

Video yourself saying the tongue twister *"Two tiny tigers take two taxis to town."*

Use bedsheets and blankets to build a tent!

T is for toothbrush. Use an old toothbrush to paint the letter t.

Evaluate: /t/

Colour the face that shows how you feel about the /t/ sound.

Got it! **Almost got it** **No, didn't get it**

Together we will continue t learn and discover new thing Let's keep moving!

Dear Parent: Date: _____

_____ does/does not fully understand the phonic sound /t/. Please continue to review at home.

Signed: _____

Dear Teacher: Date: _____

Thank you. We have reviewed the phonic sound /t/ together. My child had a chance to teach me.

Signed: _____

Reward sticker for parent or guardian goes here.

Well done!

_____
(write name here)

understands the phonic sound /t/.

Sticker for pupil goes here!

Come Back Tam!

CHEETAH Puttrrrrr Publishing
presents
Come Back Tam!
Level 2
Set 2,
Book 15

Bernadette Vidal
Paulette Trowers, JD

C-DER™
CHEETAH Decodable
& Early Readers

Let us read book 15,
Come Back, Tam!

CHEETAH® train loves a song, zooming as it hums along.
Ryan runs around. The train is rumbling on the ground.
Can you guess which sound is next?

Find an instrument, then play and sing along using the lyrics above!

Practise my sound while you look in a mirror!

The /r/ sound is on the way to town.
The CHEETAH® train is slowing down.

Concept: phonic sound /r/

The /r/ sound can appear at the start, in the middle or at the end of a word.

run

ride

round

3

three

carrot

fairy

4

four

our

after

Robin and the Rat

Robin the rooster ran around the room with a broom.

"Why are you running?" Sam asked.

"I saw a rat running around the room. I am going to race after the rat and ask it to stop running around the room."

"The rat will not stop running," said Sam. "He is looking for his rocket."

Suddenly, the rat raced outside where a rocket stood in the rain. Robin watched the red rocket take off with a roar. "You cannot catch me!" called the rat, riding the rocket across the sky.

Apply: /r/

Say the words for each picture. Tick (✓) the pictures that have the /r/ sound.

☐    ☐    ☐

☐    ☐    ☐

Practise writing the letter r.

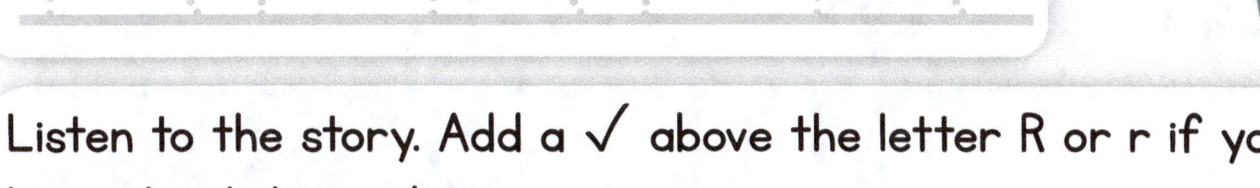

Curl your tongue slightly back without touching the top. Splendid!

Listen to the story. Add a ✓ above the letter R or r if you hear the /r/ sound.

Roy the Rabbit

Roy, the red rabbit, loves to run.

After the rain, he races in the roaring river.

His fur gets wet, but Roy doesn't care.

He just loves to run around and race.

/r/ sound = _____

Rr

My Word Wall

(from the story *Ras the Rat*)

Ras	rat	run	rug

ram	Ron	the

can	on	from	a

with	and

Colour the words you know.
You read and roar with pride!

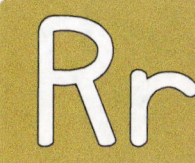

My Word Work Mats*

Say & tap · Map (sounds) · Graph (letters) · Check · Write it

Rr

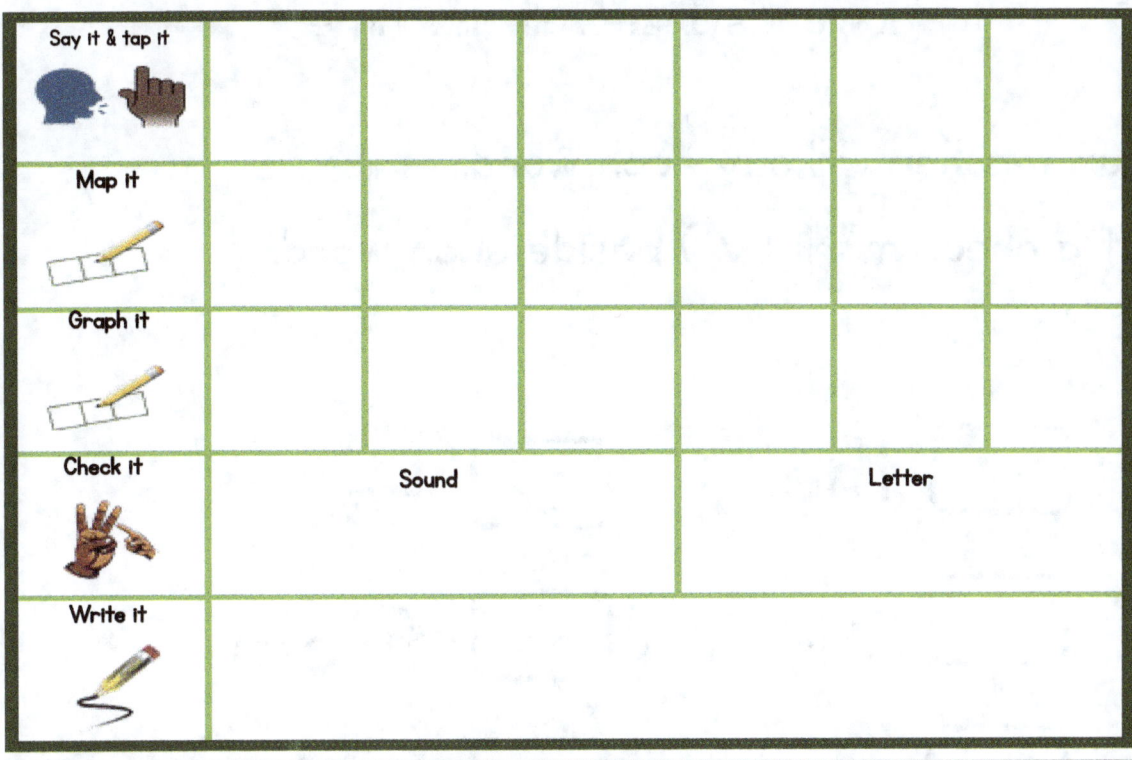

Say it & tap it					
Map it					
Graph it					
Check it	Sound			Letter	
Write it					

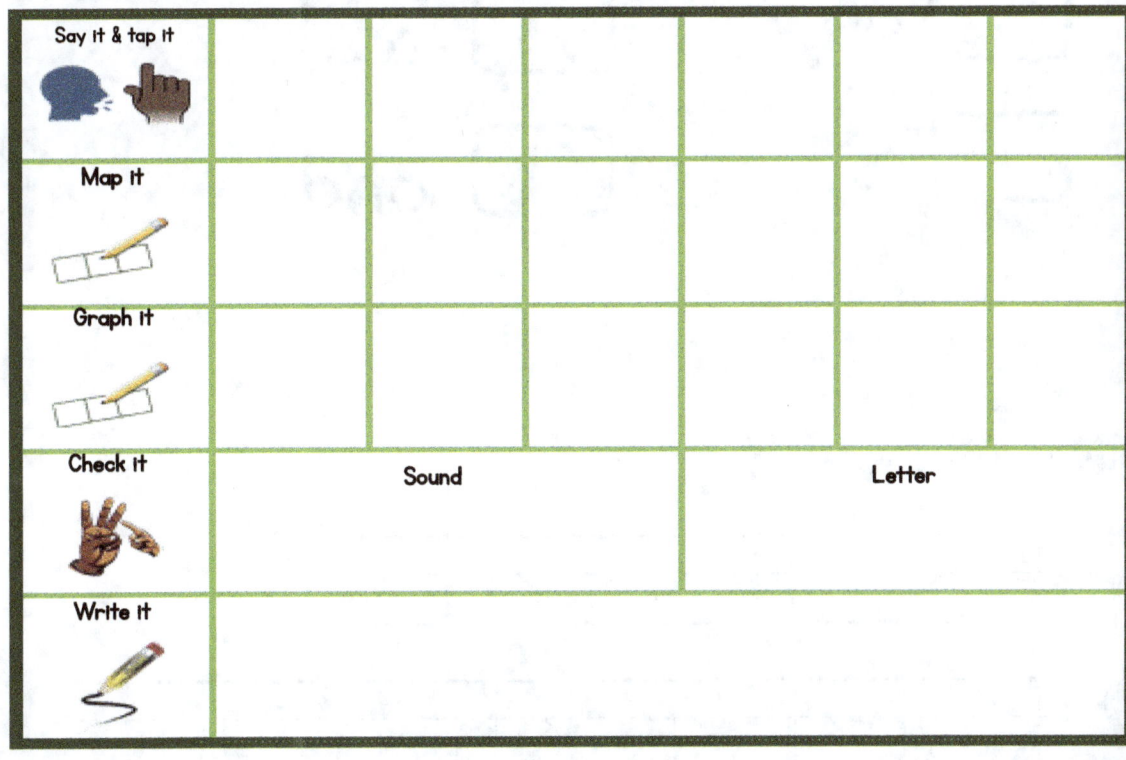

Say it & tap it					
Map it					
Graph it					
Check it	Sound			Letter	
Write it					

Put a ♥ above any part of the word that is tricky.

Get more words from C-DER® book 15, *Come Back, Tam!*
Use your poster to learn the **-ar** word family.

Sight Words Activity

(words I see all the time)

Your teacher will say each word.

Put a check mark (✓) beside each word.

☐ the   ☐ he

☐ can   ☐ from

☐ on   ☐ with

☐ a   ☐ and

Sentences:

1. Ras is a rat.

2. Ras ran on a rug.

3. Ras ran with Ron.

I can read with you!

JamDER+
Jamaican Decodable & Early Readers

Name: _____

Ras the Rat
By Paul Law

Ras the rat can run. Ras can run on a rug. He can run with a rag. He can run from a ram. Ras can run with Ron. Ras and Ron run on the rug. Run, Ras! Run!

Answer these questions:

1. Who are the characters in the story?
2. Where did Ras and Ron run?
3. Who wrote this story? What is the title?
4. Can you read the last three words the way your teacher does?

My Reading Record

Reading #1: ____ WCPM
Reading #2: ____ WCPM
Reading #3: ____ WCPM

Practise: /r/

With a friend, play the game *Roam the Room*. You each have 3 minutes to collect as many objects with the /r/ sound as you can find!

Paint a rainbow. Which of the colours contain the /r/ sound?

R is for rice. Draw an outline of the letter r, then stick rice on it.

Reread the C-DER® book, *Come Back, Tam!* Sort the /r/ words into groups according to whether the sound is at the start, in the middle or at the end.

Task: Create your own story about a rabbit.
Step 1: Think about what happens in your story – where does the rabbit go, and who does it meet?
Step 2: Record your story using the **CHEETAH®** Reading Partner. Listen to how it sounds.
Step 3: Use your recording to create your own book – add sentences, drawings, and a title page.

R is for rock. Collect a pile of rocks and arrange them into the shape of the letter r.

135

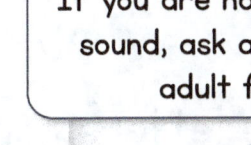

Colour the face that shows how you feel about the /r/ sound.

If you are not sure about a sound, ask a friend or an adult for help.

Got it!

Almost got it

No, didn't get it

Dear Parent: Date: _____

_____ does/does not fully understand the phonic sound /r/. Please continue to review at home.

Signed: _____

Dear Teacher: Date: _____

Thank you. We have reviewed the phonic sound /r/ together. My child had a chance to teach me.

Signed: _____

Reward sticker for parent or guardian goes here.

Well done!

Sticker for pupil goes here!

_____
(write name here)

understands the phonic sound /r/.

CHEETAH® Review

Use the letters representing the missing sounds to complete the words.

f	n	i	t	r

_ i s h   t e _ t

_ a t   p e _   c a _

CHEETAH® Review

Use the letters to make as many words as you can.

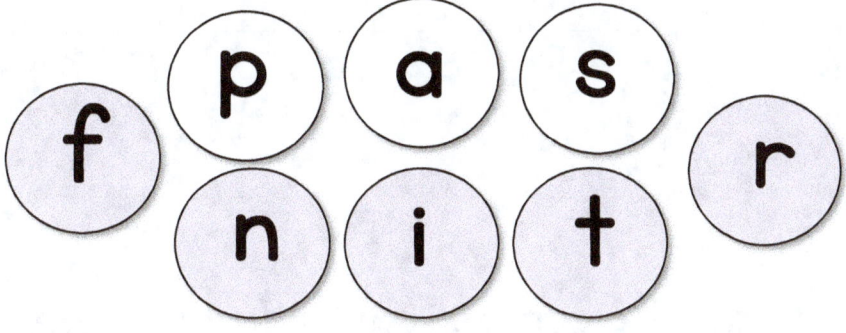

How many words did you make? Teach someone at home how to create words using letters.

CHEETAH® Review

Find the sight words in the word search.

b	i	g	r	m
f	n	d	u	g
o	g	a	n	d
u	e	s	a	f
r	t	f	l	y

and   big fly   run   get   four

Play the game *I spy with my little eye* using the /f/, /n/, short i, /t/ and /r/ sounds.

Solve the clues to complete the crossword.

Across:
3. Another word for small.
5. The boy is sitting __ the chair.

Down:
1. An insect with wings.
2. The colour of a tomato.
4. One and one make this number.

Let's create

Complete the table. Put the letters together to make words.

beginning sound	middle sound	end sound	words created
f n t r	i	t	fit, nit, tit, rit, fig, nig
		g	
		p	
		n	
		m	

List the words that you do not know the meaning of.

_____

_____

Ask an adult what they mean.

Sound out the words you have made.

Let's put together

Connect the boxes to make words from the –at word family. Write them in the given space.

s

p   -at

f

m

_____

_____

_____

_____

Knowing word families will make it easier to read and write.

Let's take apart

Spell the name of each object and write the letters of each word in the box.

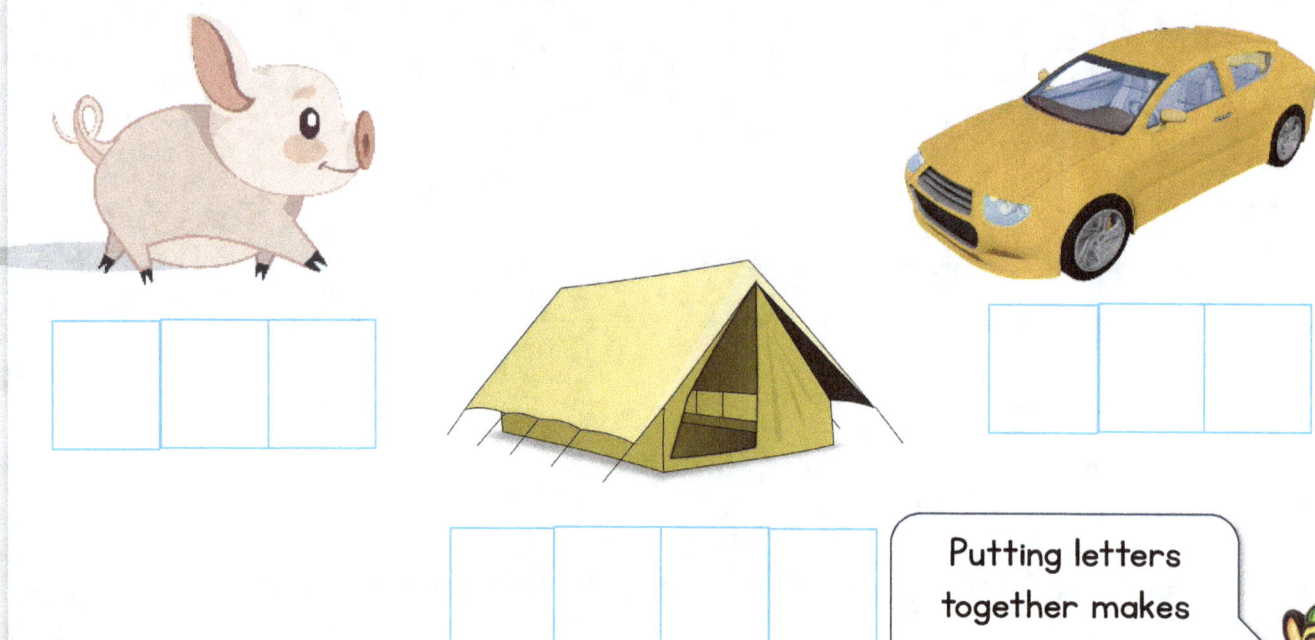

Putting letters together makes words.

Let's trace

Trace the letters to write sentences.

I see a ram.

I had a nap.

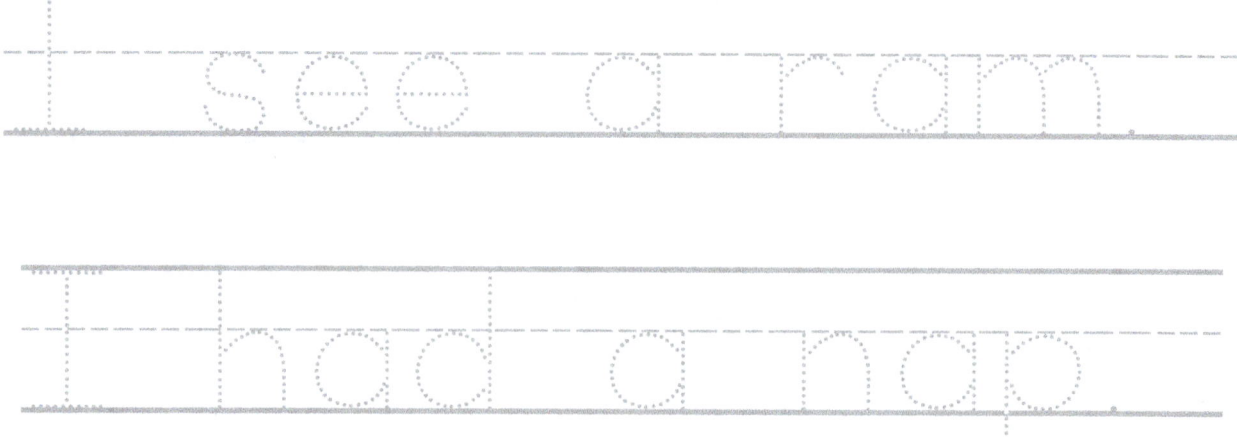

Read the sentences you have written.

NOTE: See the JamDER+ Poster Story for the story shown on the next page.

Sound and Letter Sets *: set 1: s, a, m, e, p   set 2: f, n, l, t, r

Decodable words list:

Pam, map, am, sap, pan, tan, nap, mat, Nat (name), an, sat, tap, pat, nap, pan, sit, sip, tip, tin, pit, pin, nip, met, pen, men, ten, pet, rap, rat, ref, rem, net, ram, rep, rif, rip, ran, rap, in, man, mam, fit, fin, fan, fat

NOTE: Not all these decodable words are in this story.

Sight words:

by, the, on, with a, to, and, have, can, gave**, had, on, and

*As outlined by MOESYI
** Dolch sight words used in the second grade.

Fluency test instructions

On the next page, you will find the decodable reader presented as a fluency test. Fluent readers read effortlessly, recognising words automatically and gaining meaning from what they have read. By practising fluency, the child's ability to read with accuracy and expression will get better and better.

Step 1: Read the decodable reader for the first time and see how far the child gets in one minute. Quietly note how many mistakes are made and the final word they read before the minute is up. NOTE: do not stop the child if they make a mistake.

Step 2: Write the total number of words read on the words per minute (WPM) line.

Step 3: Write the total number of mistakes made on the mistakes per minute (MPM) line.

Step 4: Subtract the mistakes per minute (MPM) from the words per minute (WPM) to calculate the words correct per minute. Write this number on the words correct per minute (WCPM) line.

Step 5: Review the mistakes made together and have the child read the test two more times to practise.

Repeat this process every day for one week following the learning of the Sets 1 and 2 sounds. Can you see the progress made?

Sets 1 and 2: Fluency Test

Note: See this CHEETAH® Poster Story with images in the Pupil's Helper book.

Pet on the Mat

Sam met Pam by the mat.	6
Pam sat on the mat with Sam.	13
A pet ran to Pam and Sam.	20
The pet sat on the mat by Sam.	28
Have a sip, Pam.	32
Can the pet sip it?	37
The pet can tip it!	42
Nip the mat	45
Rip!	46
The pet gave Pam the tin.	52
The pet had a nap on the mat	60
by Pam and Sam	64

Can you read this story?

Day 1	Day 2	Day 3	Day 4	Day 5
WPM: _____	WPM: _____	WPM: _____	WPM: _____	WPM: _____
MPM: _____	MPM: _____	MPM: _____	MPM: _____	MPM: _____
WCPM: _____	WCPM: _____	WCPM: _____	WCPM: _____	WCPM: _____

143

CHEETAH® Reward Stickers

Did you have fun? I did!

This page has been left blank so you can cut out the reward stickers.

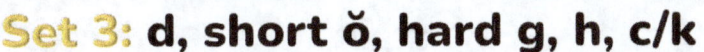

Set 3: d, short ŏ, hard g, h, c/k

Please refer to the corresponding CHEETAH® Poster Stories© and fluency test for this set's focus sounds. Additionally, the following C-DER® books are recommended for comprehension and fluency practise:

Sound	C-DER® reference	Book title
d	Set 3, book 17	Ted Disobeys
	Set 3, book 18	Nature Walk
short ŏ	Set 3, book 20	Look What I Got
hard g	Set 3, book 21	Glenda Needs Help
	Set 3, book 23	A Gift for Gary
h	Set 3, book 24	Hilda and Her Chicks
c/k	Set 3:	
	book 25	At the Kite Festival
	book 26	Time to Go
	book 27	We are Ready for Christmas
	book 28	Tam Gets in Trouble

Teaching tips*:

- the /d/ sound is a voiced stop sound, made by stopping the airflow with your tongue at the ridge behind your teeth, and then releasing it.
- the short ŏ sound is pronounced 'ah' as in 'stop.'
- make sure the hard /g/ sound is 'g' as in 'gold.'
- the /h/ sound is not voiced. Make a 'h' sound by expelling air.
- the /k/ sound (spelled, c, k, or ck) is not voiced. Block air from the throat with the back of your tongue, then release it.

Wah gwaan? Do you remember my name? I am here to guide you to the highest heights in reading. The sky is the limit. Let's soar together!

Did You Know? #2

These 11 words
make up about 25% of
the words children use.

the

and

it

it

is

at

to

on

at

up

you

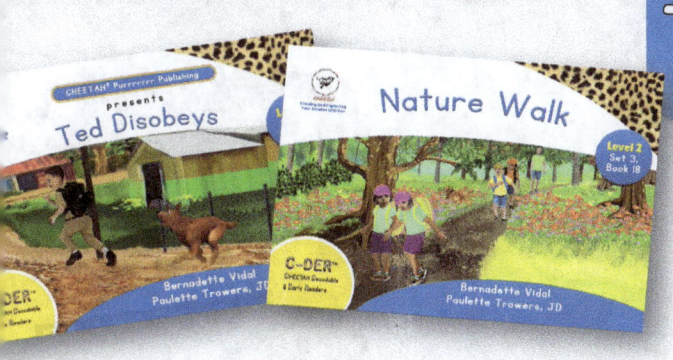

The /d/ sound

Ted Disobeys
Bernadette Vidal
Paulette Trowers, JD
Nature Walk
Level 2
Set 3,
Book 18
Bernadette Vidal
Paulette Trowers, JD

Let's read together books 17, *Ted Disobeys*, and 18, *Nature Walk*.

CHEETAH® train loves a song, zooming as it hums along.
Daisy loves a dancing beat, drumming music on her seat.
Can you guess which sound is next?

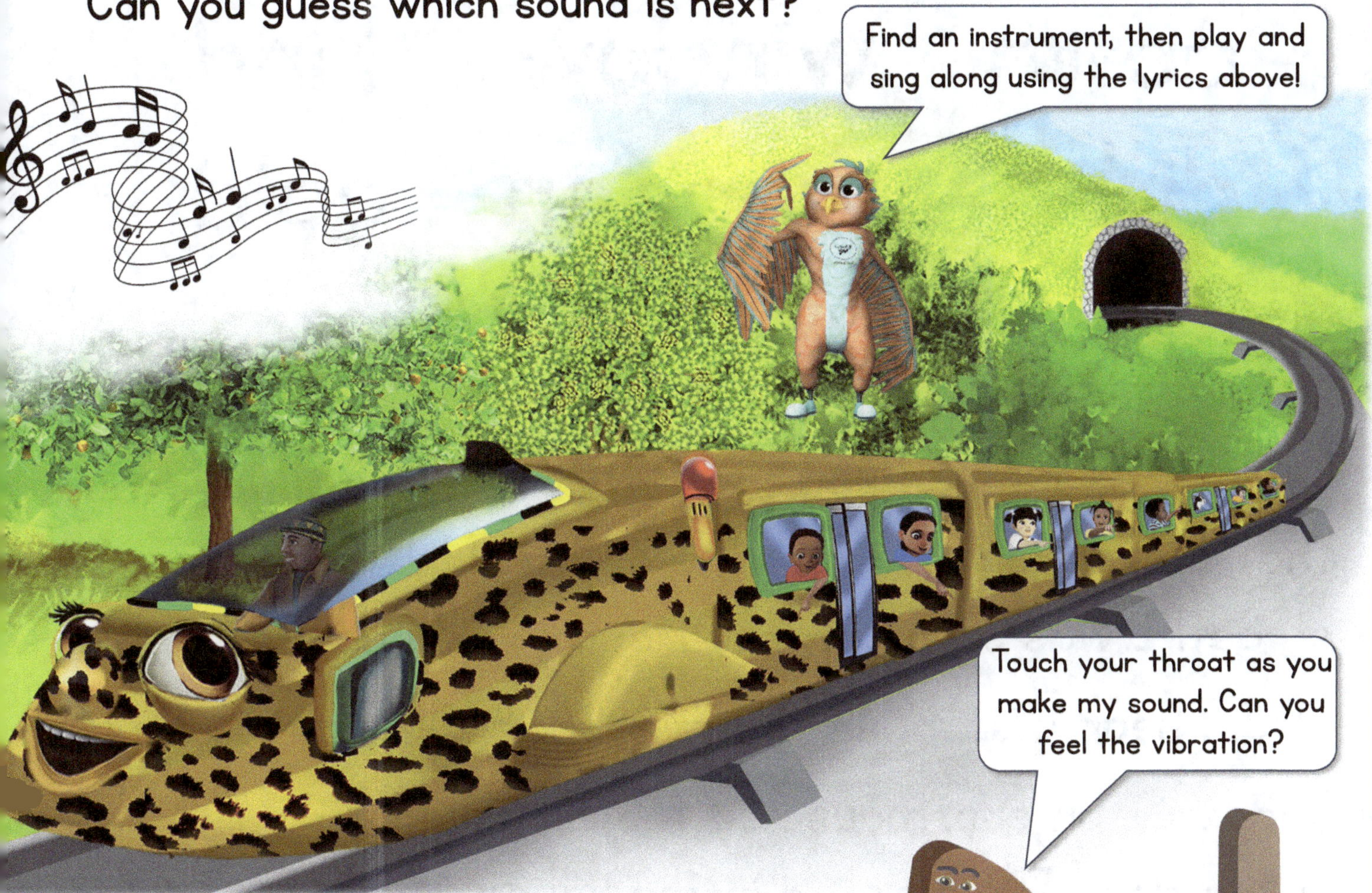
Find an instrument, then play and sing along using the lyrics above!
Touch your throat as you make my sound. Can you feel the vibration?

The /d/ sound is on the way to town.
The CHEETAH® train is slowing down.

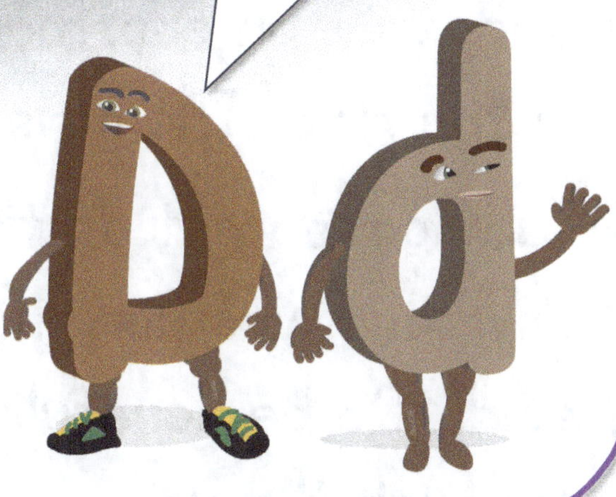

Concept: phonic sound /d/

Dd

The /d/ sound can appear at the start, in the middle or at the end of a word.

dish

down

did

spi**d**er

win**d**ow

woo**d**en

hea**d**

fin**d**

col**d**

Daisy and the Dinosaur

One day, Daisy Duck rang Pam's doorbell.

"I am glad I found you," said Daisy. "I had a daydream that a big red dinosaur gave you a ride down the street! I was sure the daydream would come true!"

"I did hear a sound in the middle of the night," said Pam.

Suddenly, an enormous red foot crashed down in the mud. The girls hid in the house.

Pam looked out of the window and saw that the dinosaur was dancing. "I am going outside," she said. "Do be careful," said Daisy. Pam dived through the door and danced toward the disco.

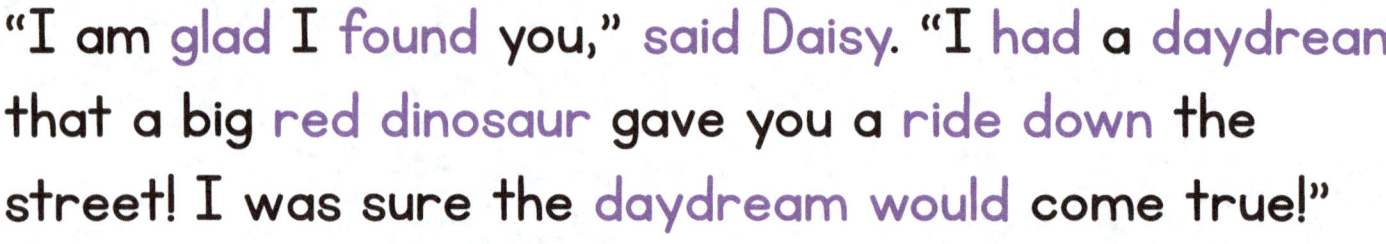

Apply: /d/

Listen to the words for each picture. Draw a line from the pictures with a /d/ sound to the letter Dd.

Dd

Practise writing the letter *d.*

Tap your tongue behind your top teeth and turn on your voice. You can do this!

Listen to the story. Circle the letter D or d if you hear the /d/ sound.

Ted in Bed

Ted had a big red bed.

He would jump on it until he was fed.

His mum said, "Off to bed, Ted!"

Ted climbed into bed and rested his head.

/D/ sound = _____

My Word Wall

(from the story *Das at the Dam*)

Dan	dad	dam	Das
	his	went	let
play	that	saw	the
	sad	and	had

Colour the words you know.
Do your best every day!

151

My Word Work Mats*

Say & tap · Map (sounds) · Graph (letters) · Check · Write it

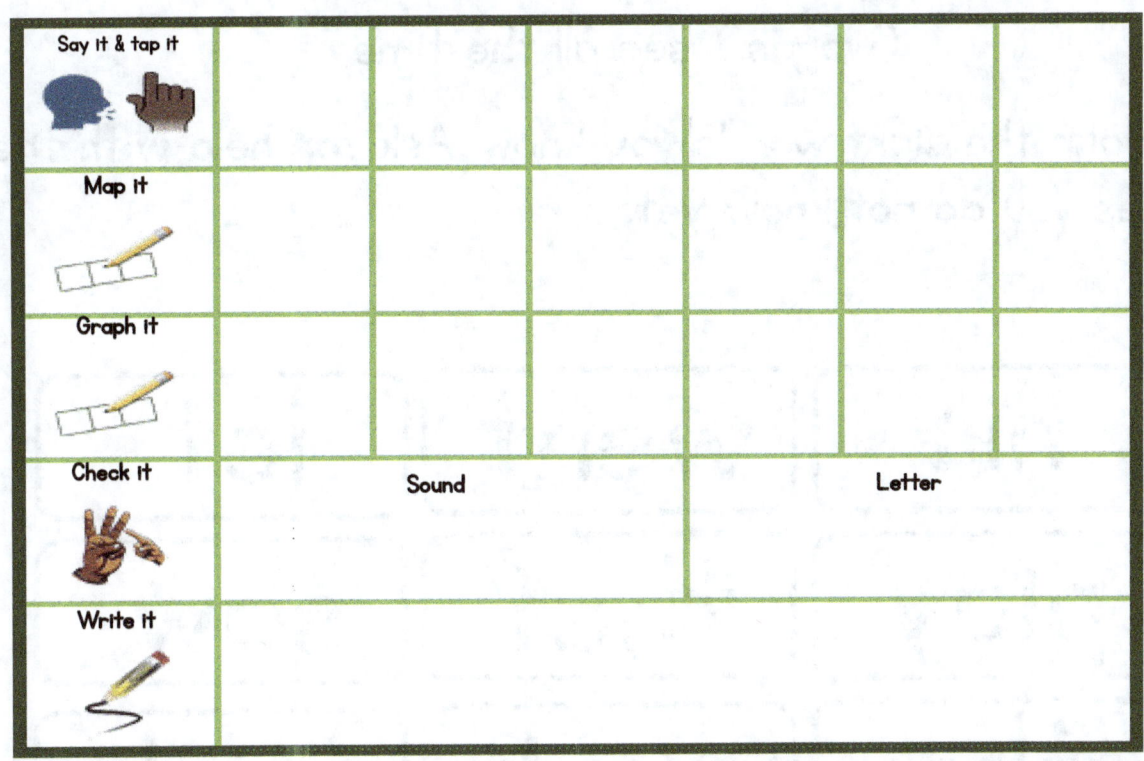

Dd

Say it & tap it

Map it

Graph it

Check it — Sound — Letter

Write it

Say it & tap it

Map it

Graph it

Check it — Sound — Letter

Write it

Put a 🧡 above any part of the word that is tricky.

Get more words from C–DER® books 17, *Ted Disobeys*, and 18, *Nature Walk*. Use your poster to learn the **-ad** word family.

*Adapted and modified by CHEETAH® Toys & More, LLC for inclusion in this educational work.

Sight Words Activity

(words I see all the time)

Colour the sight words you know. Ask for help with the ones you do not know yet.

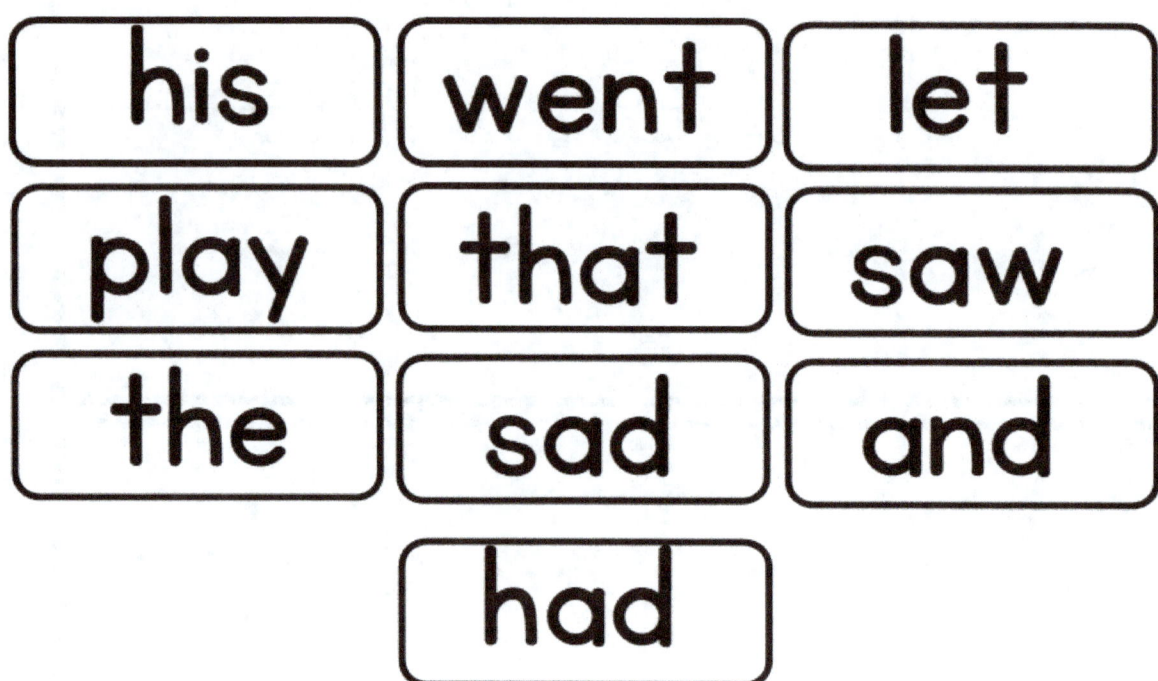

his	went	let
play	that	saw
the	sad	and
had		

Sentences:

1. Dad saw Das.

2. Dan saw the net.

3. Das was sad.

I can read with you!

Dd

Name: _____

Das at the Dam

Dan and his dad went to the dam. They saw Das and her dad at the dam. Das was sad. Dad said to Dan, "Let Das dip the net." Das did dip the net in the dam.

Dan and his dad saw Das at play. Das and her dad had fun that day. So did Dan and his dad.

Portland Dam

Answer these questions:

1. Who are the characters in the story?

2. Where did the story take place?

3. What did Das do with the net?

4. What does dam mean as used in the story?

My Reading Record

Reading #1: ____ WCPM
Reading #2: ____ WCPM
Reading #3: ____ WCPM

Practise: /d/

D is for dots! Use a cotton bud to paint dots in the shape of the letter *d*.

Look through magazines for the letter *d*. Cut it out whenever you see it. On a piece of paper, stick all the lowercase d's together and all the capital D's together.

Read the C-DER® book, *Ted Disobeys*. Look for /d/ words in the story. Use the CHEETAH® letters to spell the words out. Can you read them all?

Use the CHEETAH® CVC puzzle pieces to create words in the *-ad* and *-ed* word families.

Use the iCHEETAH© to create a short story based on the class's choice. Let pupils suggest and vote on the topic, then listen together. Afterward, ask one or two quick questions to check understanding.

Evaluate: /d/

Colour the face that shows how you feel about the /d/ sound.

I am impressed by how much you are learning! Come fly with me to the next sound.

Got it!

Almost got it

No, didn't get it

Dear Parent: Date: _____

_____ does/does not fully understand the phonic sound /d/. Please continue to review at home.

Signed: _____

Dear Teacher: Date: _____

Thank you. We have reviewed the phonic sound /d/ together. My child had a chance to teach me.

Signed: _____

Reward sticker for parent or guardian goes here.

You did it!

_____
(write name here)

understands the phonic sound /d/.

Sticker for pupil goes here!

Let's read together book 20,
Look What I Got.

CHEETAH® train loves a song, zooming as it hums along.
An ox is on a box! He is dancing in his orange socks.
Can you guess which sound is next?

Find an instrument, then play and sing along using the lyrics above!

Can you say my sound three times?

The short ŏ sound is on the way to town.
The CHEETAH® train is slowing down.

Concept: phonic sound short ŏ

Short Oŏ

The short ŏ sound can appear at the start or in the middle of a word.

ox   box

on   stop

octopus   not

The Ox and the Frog

Rod the frog hopped to the forest to sit upon a log. It was very hot, and a horrible, thick fog fell upon the forest. All the animals were soon gone. A fox climbed to the top of a rock to see if he could spot them over the fog. "Do not worry, Fox! Stay with us, and we will not stop looking until the fog moves from the forest."

All the animals sang, and when the fog was gone, Rod the frog was a little sad.

"What is wrong?" asked Oliver the ox. "Did it scare you to be lost in the fog?"

"It is not that," said Rod. "I am sad we stopped singing!"

158

Apply: short ŏ

Say the name of each picture. (Circle) the pictures that have the short ŏ sound.

Make your mouth round and open.
Well done!

Practise writing the letter o.

Listen to the story. <u>Underline</u> the letter O or o if you hear  the short ŏ sound.

Bob the Dog

Bob the dog got a job in a shop.

The shop had lots of socks and tops.

On his day off, he shot out of bed.

"I am off to have some fun!" said Bob.

short ŏ sound = _____

My Word Wall

(from the story *Odd Man Otto*)

short
Oŏ

oh	Otto	odd	lot
pot	hot	no	
who	do	on	see
to	old	from	over

Colour the words you know.
You are on a roll, rockstar!

My Word Work Mats*

Say & tap · Map (sounds) · Graph (letters) · Check · Write it

short **Oŏ**

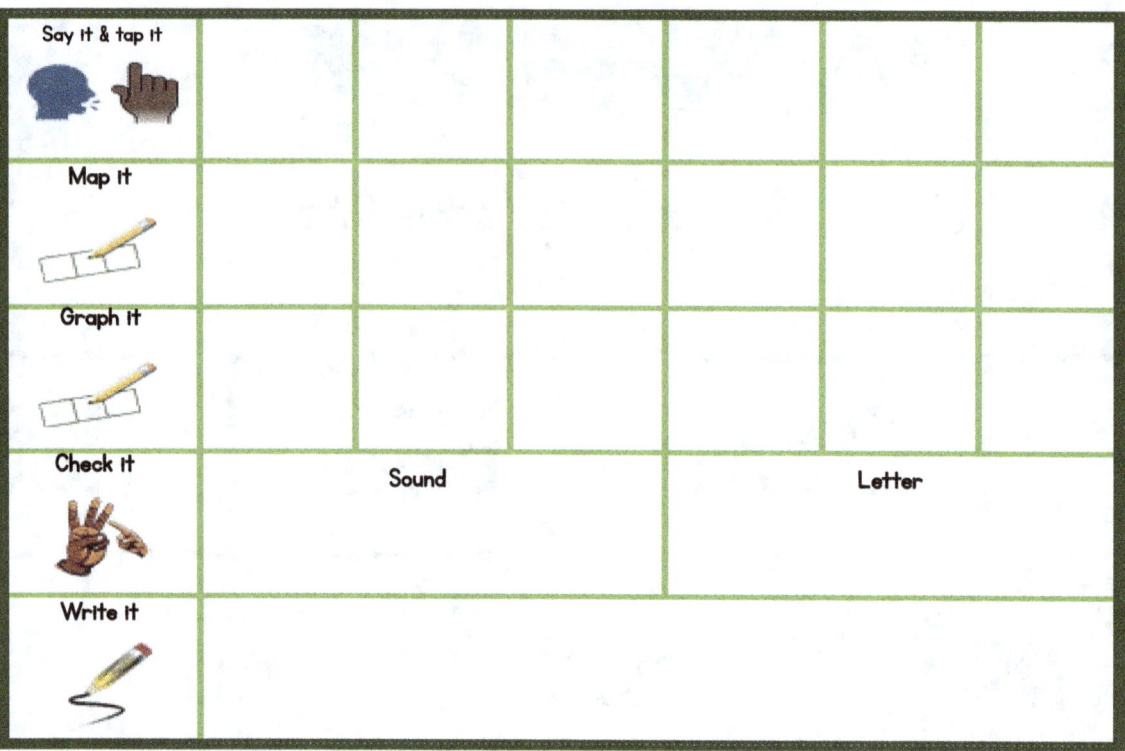

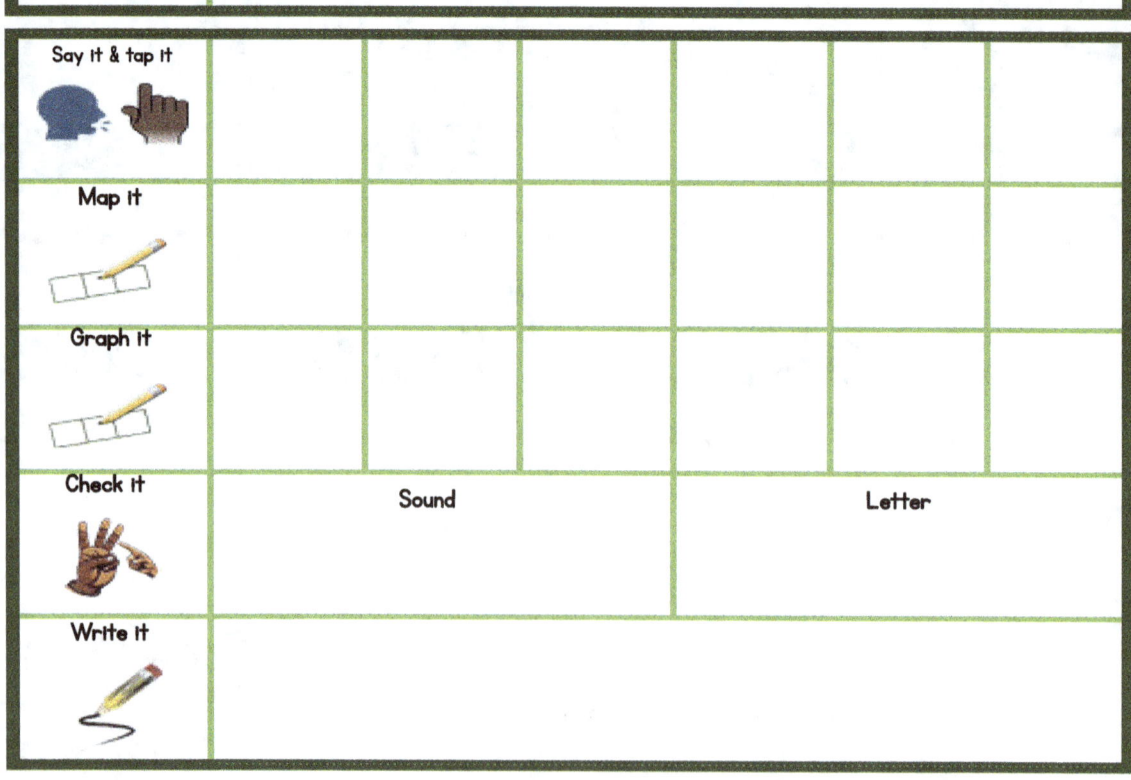

Put a 🧡 above any part of the word that is tricky.

Get more words from C-DER® book 20, *Look What I Got!* Use your poster to learn the **-ot** word family.

*Adapted and modified by CHEETAH® Toys & More, LLC for inclusion in this educational work.

Sight Words Activity

(words I see all the time)

Remember the cheetah® chant©!

no _____

who _____

do _____

on _____

see _____

to _____

old _____

from_____

over _____

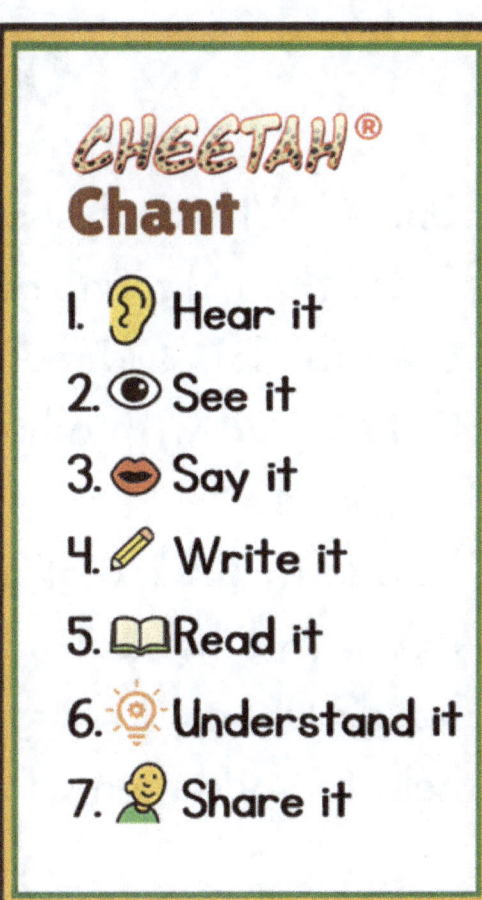

CHEETAH®
Chant

1. Hear it
2. See it
3. Say it
4. Write it
5. Read it
6. Understand it
7. Share it

Sentences:

1. I see an old man.

2. I will get help.

I can read with you!

Name: _____

Old Man Otto

Oh, no! Who do I see? Otto, the old man from over the lot. Old man Otto is odd with a hot pot on his head.
Is odd man Otto off to jog, with a hot pot on his head? Oh, no! I will get help for odd man Otto.

Answer these questions:

1. What do you think Otto was trying to do with the pot?

2. Why should you get help for him?

3. Can you read the story the way your teacher read it?

My Reading Record

Reading #1: _____ WCPM
Reading #2: _____ WCPM
Reading #3: _____ WCPM

Practise: short ŏ

Use the CHEETAH® Reading Partner to calculate selected pupils' reading levels. This activity may be done over several classroom sessions.

Dip the top of a round cup or container in paint. Use it to print the letter o.

Read the C-DER® book, *Look What I Got.* Make a list of the short o words you see. Be careful! Not every word with the letter o has a short ŏ sound.

O is for orange. How many orange objects can you find and photograph?

Make short ŏ words using the CHEETAH® CVC puzzle pieces.

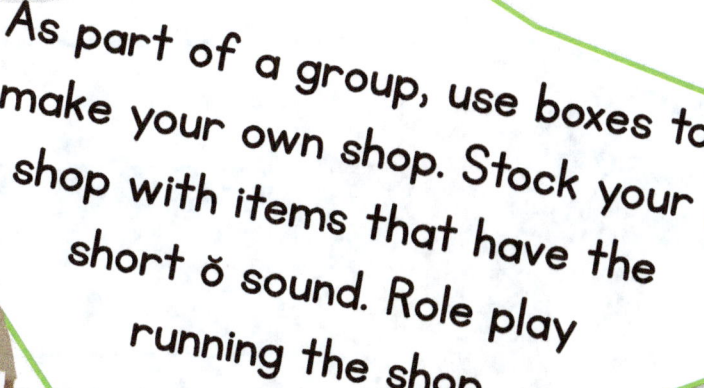

As part of a group, use boxes to make your own shop. Stock your shop with items that have the short ŏ sound. Role play running the shop.

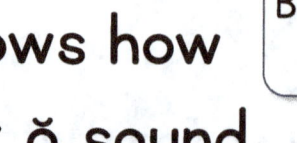

Evaluate: short ŏ

Colour the face that shows how you feel about the short ŏ sound.

Be proud of yourself for spreading your wings!

Got it!

Almost got it

No, didn't get it

Dear Parent: Date: _____

_____ does/does not fully understand the short ŏ phonic sound. Please continue to review at home.

Signed: _____

Dear Teacher: Date: _____

Thank you. We have reviewed the short ŏ phonic sound together. My child had a chance to teach me.

Signed: _____

Reward sticker for parent or guardian goes here.

Good work!

Sticker for pupil goes here!

_____

(write name here)

understands the phonic sound short ŏ.

Glenda Needs Help
A Gift for Gary

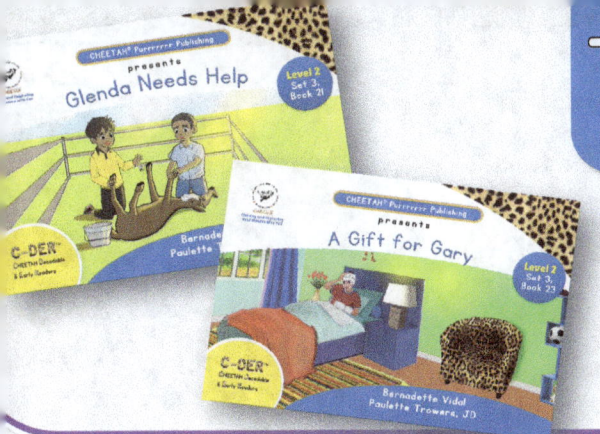

The hard /g/ sound

Let us read books 21, *Glenda Needs Help*, and 23, *A Gift for Gary*.

CHEETAH® train loves a song, zooming as it hums along.
A goat is eating grass, grinning as the train goes past.
Can you guess which sound is next?

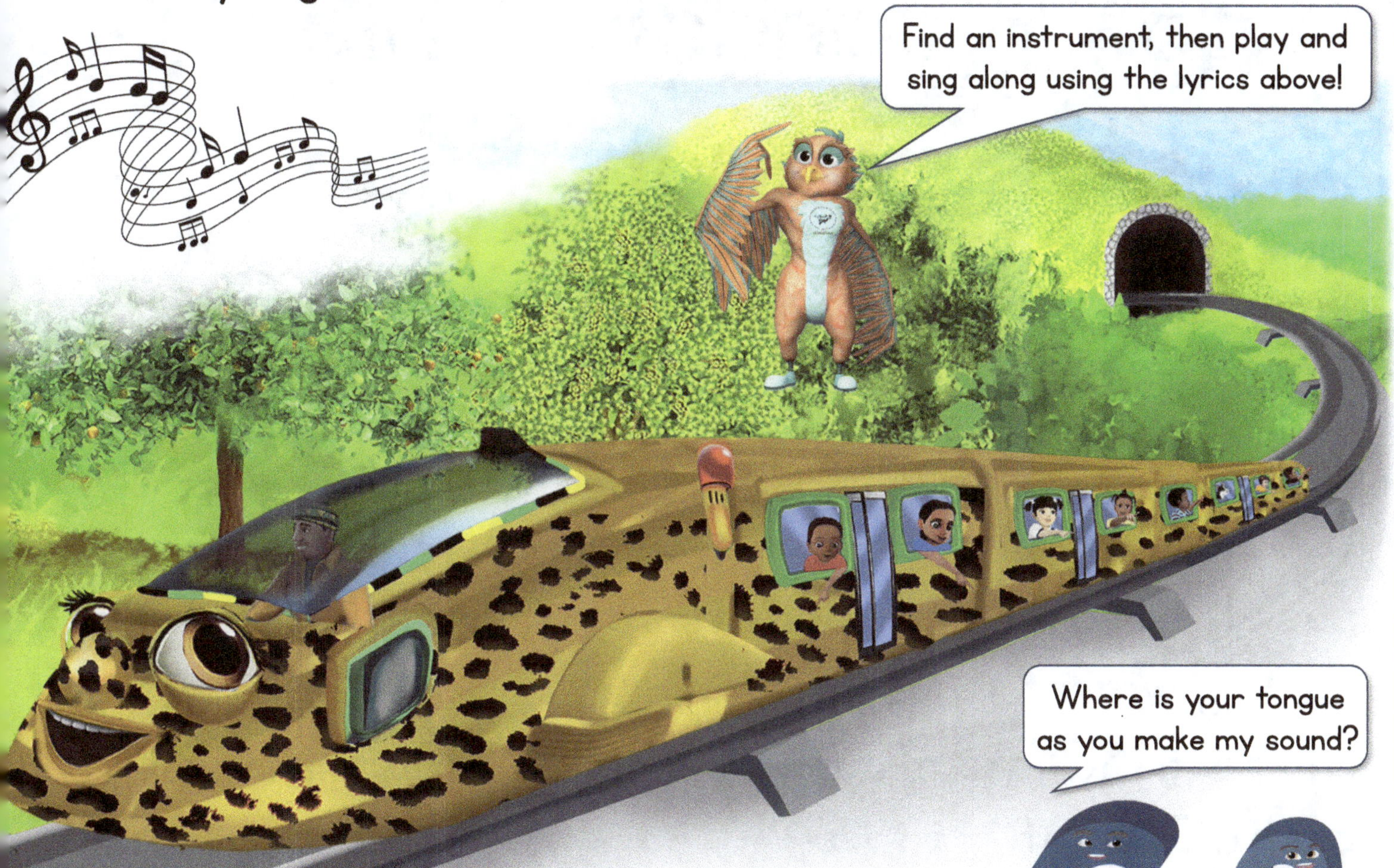
Find an instrument, then play and sing along using the lyrics above!
Where is your tongue as you make my sound?

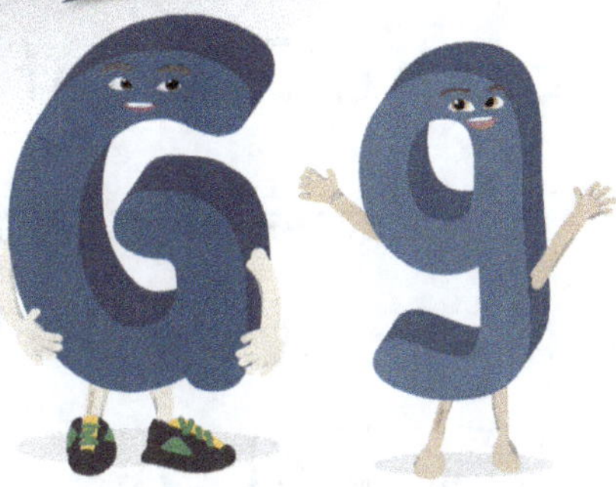
G g

The hard /g/ sound is on the way to town.
The CHEETAH® train is slowing down.

Concept: phonic sound hard /g/ 🔊

The hard /g/ sound can appear at the start, in the middle or at the end of a word.

gate	sugar	frog
go	anger	big
get	began	leg

Gabby the Goat

Gabby was a goat who loved to gallop. One day, Gabby 🔊 had a great big game board to deliver to Gail the gorilla. Gabby could not wait to get going through the gate and past the bog. She galloped over the golden fields, past a gushing waterfall and a giggling gecko. She ran so fast that she began to take off from the ground. Soon she was flying past a flock of seagulls.

"You are such a good goat," said Gail the gorilla when Gabby gave her the gift. "But I did not know that goats could fly!"

"This is the first time!" said Gabby. "I hope I fly again!"

Apply: hard /g/

Listen to the word for each picture. Put a cross (X) through the pictures that do **NOT** have the hard /g/ sound.

Practise writing the letter g.

Lift the back of your tongue and feel you voice hum.

Great!

Listen to the story. Add a ✓ above the letter G or g if you hear the /g/ sound.

Greedy Gabby

Gabby the goat loves to gallop.

She goes around the garden,

gobbling up the green grass.

Goodness, Gabby is a greedy goat!

/g/ sound = _____

My Word Wall

(from the story *Gaga the Frog*)

gate	get	Gaga	grin
gum	grab	big
bag	egg	sag	nag
went	she	had	again

Colour the words you know.
You keep climbing higher. Good job!

169

My Word Work Mats*

Say & tap · Map (sounds) · Graph (letters) · Check · Write it

hard Gg

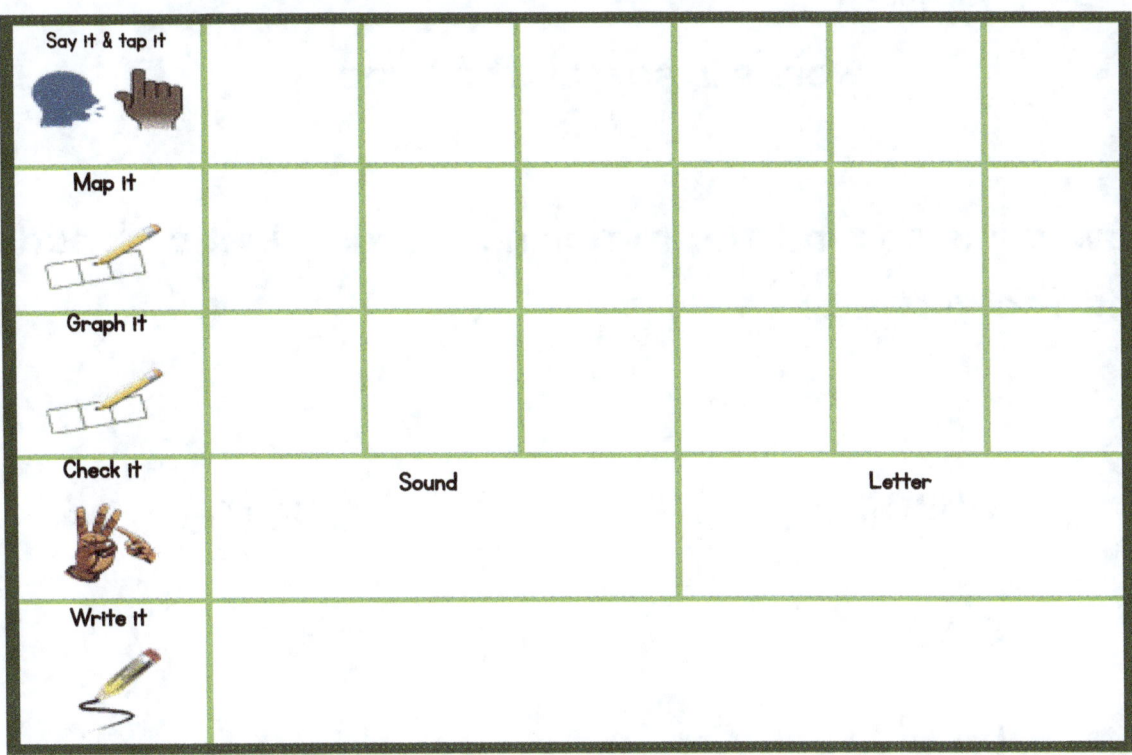

Say it & tap it					
Map it					
Graph it					
Check it	Sound			Letter	
Write it					

Say it & tap it					
Map it					
Graph it					
Check it	Sound			Letter	
Write it					

Put a ♥ above any part of the word that is tricky.

Get more words from C-DER® books 21, *Glenda Needs Help*, and 23, *A Gift for Gary*. Use your poster to learn the **-eg** word family.

*Adapted and modified by CHEETAH® Toys & More, LLC for inclusion in this educational work.

Sight Words Activity

(words I see all the time)

Draw a line to find the matching words. One is already done for you

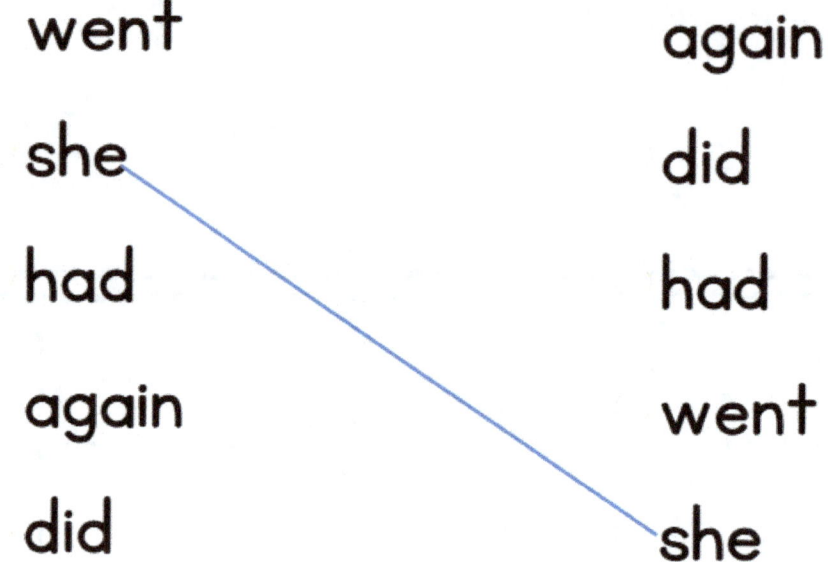

went	again
she	did
had	had
again	went
did	she

Sentences:

1. Gaga is a frog.

2. An egg is in the bag.

I can read with you!

Name: _____

Gaga the frog

Gaga the Frog went to the gate. She went to get a big bag. The bag had sugar. The bag had an egg. The sugar and egg sat in the bag with a sag. Gaga did grab the bag but lost her grip. She did drop the bag. Sugar and egg went on her leg, but Gaga did not nag.

Answer these questions:

1. What was inside Gaga's bag?
2. What happened when Gaga lost her grip?
3. What is the story mostly about?
4. What do you think will happen next? Read the rest of the story:
   Gaga had a grin.
   Gaga will go to the gate again.
   Is your prediction correct?

My Reading Record

Reading #1: ____ WCPM
Reading #2: ____ WCPM
Reading #3: ____ WCPM

Practise: hard /g/

Use the microphone to sing the *CHEETAH®* hard /g/ sound song. While two pupils sing, the others act out the words using their *CHEETAH® Sing and Act Songbook.*

G is for green. Get green objects and put them into a bag. How many objects did you find?

Read the C-DER® book, *Glenda Needs Help.* Make a tally chart of how many times you see each hard /g/ word in the story.

Plant grass seeds in a pot. Photograph the seeds each day to record their growth.

G is for game. Choose a game to play with a friend.

Count the legs! Look at animal toys and videos of animals. How many legs do they have?

Go into a garden and help an adult to dig and care for the plants and flowers.

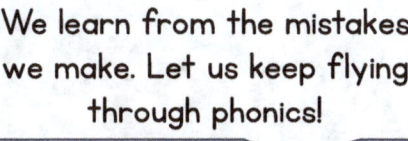

valuate: hard /g/

Colour the face that shows how you feel about the hard /g/ sound.

We learn from the mistakes we make. Let us keep flying through phonics!

Got it!

Almost got it

No, didn't get it

Dear Parent: Date: _____

_____ does/does not fully understand the phonic sound hard /g/. Please continue to review at home.

Signed: _____

Dear Teacher: Date: _____

Thank you. We have reviewed the phonic sound hard /g/ together. My child had a chance to teach me.

Signed: _____

Reward sticker for parent or guardian goes here.

Well done!

_____
(write name here)

understands the phonic sound hard /g/.

Sticker for pupil goes here!

Level 2
Set 3,
Book 24

CHEETAH® Purrrrrr Publishing

presents

Hilda and Her Chicks

Bernadette Vidal
Paulette Trowers, JD

C-DER™
CHEETAH Decodable
& Early Readers

Let us read book 24,
Hilda and Her Chicks.

CHEETAH® train loves a song, zooming as it hums along.
There is Hilda on her horse! She is happy as she rides the course!
Can you guess which sound is next?

Find an instrument, then play and sing along using the lyrics above!

Hold your hand before your mouth as you make my sound. What do you notice?

The /h/ sound is on the way to town.
The CHEETAH® train is slowing down.

Concept: phonic sound /h/

Hh

The /h/ sound can appear at the start or in the middle of a word.

hat

help

here

grasshopper

behind

unhappy

Harry the Hamster

Harry was a hamster, but he thought he was a horse. He would hurry here, there, and everywhere.

"Watch me run!" Harry would say and hurry over the hills, leaving all his friends behind. One day he entered a horse race, but all the horses laughed at him.

"How do you expect to be faster than a horse?" the horses asked Harry. "You do not have a chance!"

But Harry smiled because he had a lucky hat that helped his feet hurry.

At the end of the race, Harry was so far ahead of the horses, he was home for tea before they finished!

Apply: /h/

Say the name of each object aloud. Colour the things that begin with the letter H.

Practise writing the letter *h*.

Open your mouth and breathe out softly. Hooray!

Listen to the story. Circle the letter H or h if you hear the /h/ sound.

Henry the Horse

Henry the horse lived on a hill.

He had a hobby of hopping high.

"Will today be a happy day of hopping?"

He would ask himself each day as he hopped.

/h/ sound = _____

177

Hh

My Word Wall

(from the story *Han the Grasshopper*)

Han	hops	hums	happy

home	hot	ham

hat	hide	big	in

your	when	my

Colour the words you know.
You are a good and growing reader!

My Word Work Mats*

Say & tap · Map (sounds) · Graph (letters) · Check · Write it

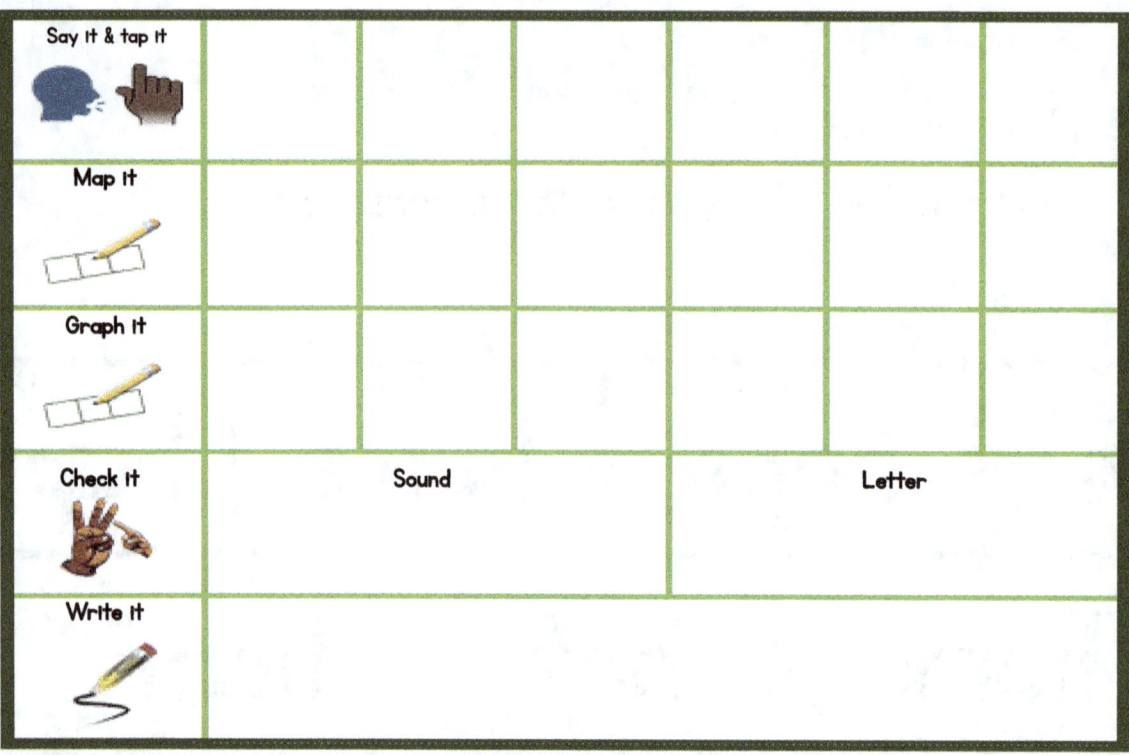

Hh

Put a ♥ above any part of the word that is tricky.

Get more words from C-DER® book 24, *Hilda and Her Chicks*. Use your poster to learn the **-op** word family.

*Adapted and modified by CHEETAH® Toys & More, LLC for inclusion in this educational work.

Sight Words Activity

(words I see all the time)

Remember the Cheetah® Chant©

big _____

in _____

your _____

when_____

my _____

Chant

1. Hear it
2. See it
3. Say it
4. Write it
5. Read it
6. Understand it
7. Share it

Sentences:

1. I am happy.

2. Han has a big hat.

I can read with you!

Name: _____

Hh

Han the Grasshopper

Han hops, Han hums.

Han, the grasshopper, is happy.

He has hot ham, and he has
a big hat. Han has a home.

Hide, Han. Hide in your
home when the sun is hot.
Han is oh so happy at home. Oh, my!

Answer these questions:

1. What does Han do at home?

2. What food does Han have?

3. Can you read the story like a storyteller?

My Reading
Record

Reading #1: _____ WCPM
Reading #2: _____ WCPM
Reading #3: _____ WCPM

Practise: /h/

Make a paper hat. Decorate your hat with the letter *h*.

Use the iCHEETAH© to play a reggae ABC song while pupils hop and dance to the rhythm.

Read the C-DER® book, *Hilda and Her Chicks*. Draw Hilda the hen with her chicks. Write a sentence to describe your picture. How many /h/ words does it have?

H is for home. Take photos of your home and the homes of people you know. With an adult, prepare a presentation to share with the class.

Hop along a trail outside, making the /h/ sound as you hop!

H is for hide. Have an adult hide sight word cards around the room. Work with a friend to find all the words with a /h/ sound.

Evaluate: /h/

Colour the face that shows how you feel about the /h/ sound.

Got it!   Almost got it   No, didn't get it

There are people to ask for help if you need to.

Dear Parent: Date: _____

_____ does/does not fully understand the phonic sound /h/. Please continue to review at home.

Signed: _____

Dear Teacher: Date: _____

Thank you. We have reviewed the phonic sound /h/ together. My child had a chance to teach me.

Signed: _____

Reward sticker for parent or guardian goes here.

Congratulations!

_____

(write name here)

understands the phonic sound /h/.

Sticker for pupil goes here!

At the Kite Festival
Time To Go
We are Ready for Christmas
Tam Gets in Trouble

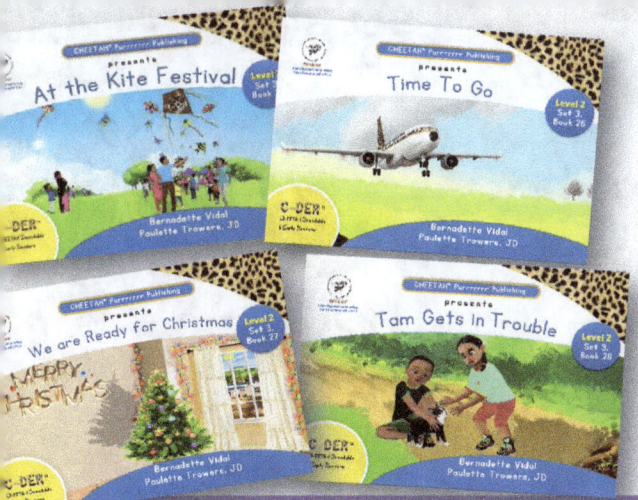

The /k/ sound

Let us read books 25, *At the Kite Festival;* 26, *Time to Go;* 27, *We Are Ready for Christmas;* and 28, *Tam Gets in Trouble.*

CHEETAH® train loves a song, zooming as it hums along.
A crab is kicking balls, clacking with its clicking claws.
Can you guess which sound is next?

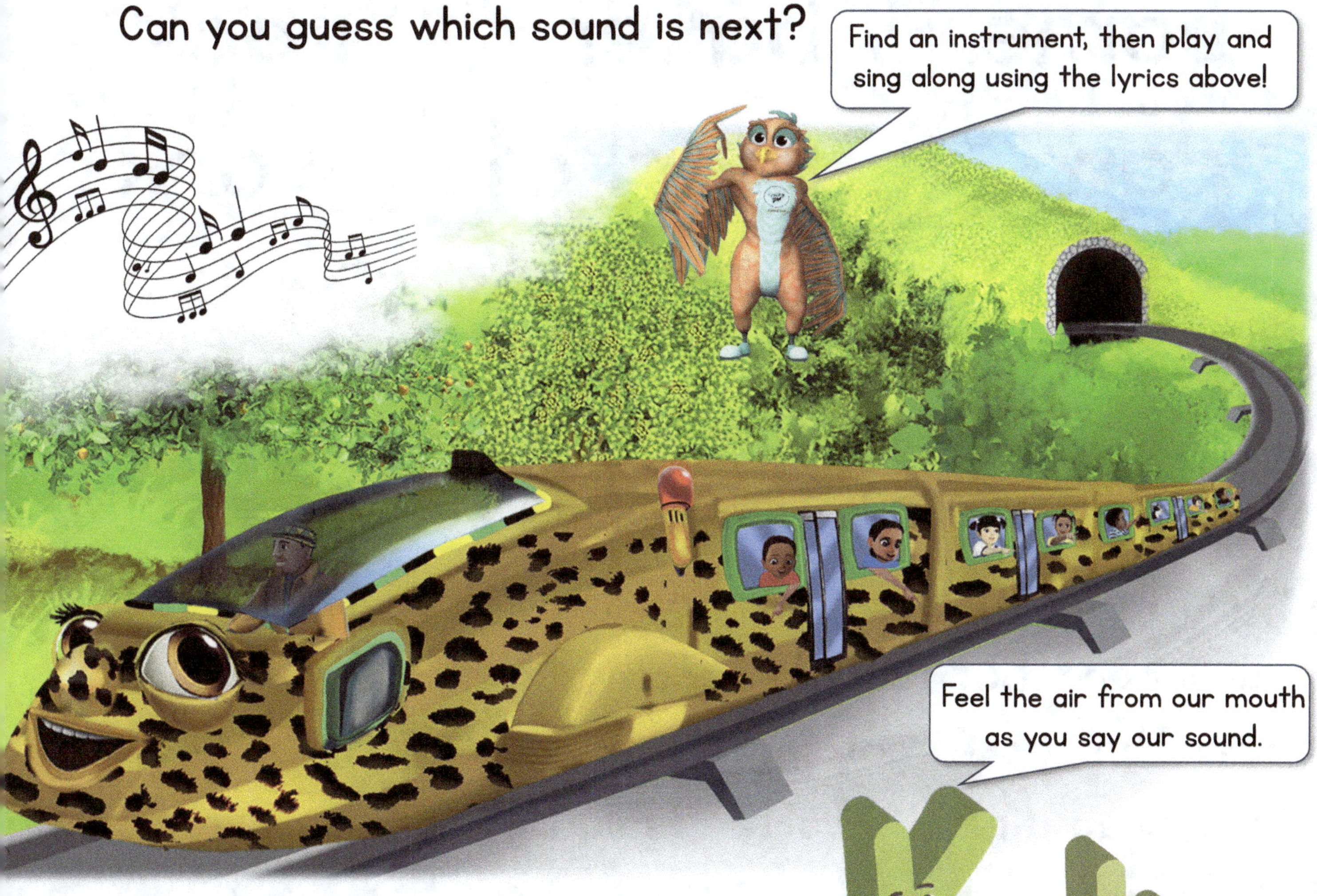
Find an instrument, then play and sing along using the lyrics above!
Feel the air from our mouth as you say our sound.
K
k

The /k/ sound is on the way to town.
The CHEETAH® train is slowing down.

Concept: phonic sound /k/

The /k/ sound can be made with a hard *c* or *k*. At the end of a word with a short vowel, the /k/ sound can also be spelled using *ck*.

kite
come
can

bacon
baker
market

picnic
rock
work

Colin and Jake

Colin was reading a book about rockets. "I like this book so much," he said. "I am going to take it to my friend Jake and ask if we can make a rocket."

"Yes, we can!" said Jake, and the kids made one out of cardboard. But the sky became dark, and it started to rain. The rocket got soggy and could not fly. "We should have used a plastic bottle," said Colin on the way home.

Jake stopped by a rock. "I know! Come to my house and let us bake a cake in the shape of a rocket." So they did, and then they ate it.

"Look," said Colin. "There is not a speck left!"

Apply: /k/

Listen to the words for each picture. Circle the ones that have the /k/ sound. The letter c can also make the /k/ sound.

Practise writing the letters *c* and *k*.

ckckck

Back of tongue up, quick puff of air.

Cracking!

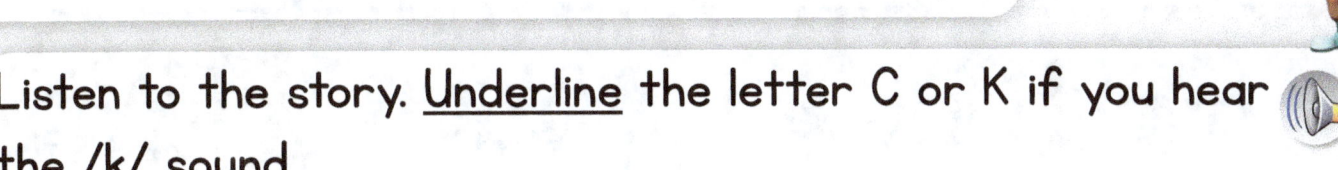

Listen to the story. <u>Underline</u> the letter C or K if you hear the /k/ sound.

Picnic with Katie

"Let us make a picnic!" Katie called to Caleb.

They put cupcakes, kiwis, and coconut water into a bag.

Next, the children biked to the park.

They sat on a rock and ate their picnic snacks.

/k/ sound = _____

My Word Wall

(from the story *Cal and Kate*)

Cal	cake	kit	kite

sack	rack	pick

and	they	from	you

know	how	said	cat

Colour the words you know.
You keep climbing higher. Good job!

187

My Word Work Mats*

Say & tap · Map (sounds) · Graph (letters) · Check · Write it

Set 3

Kk

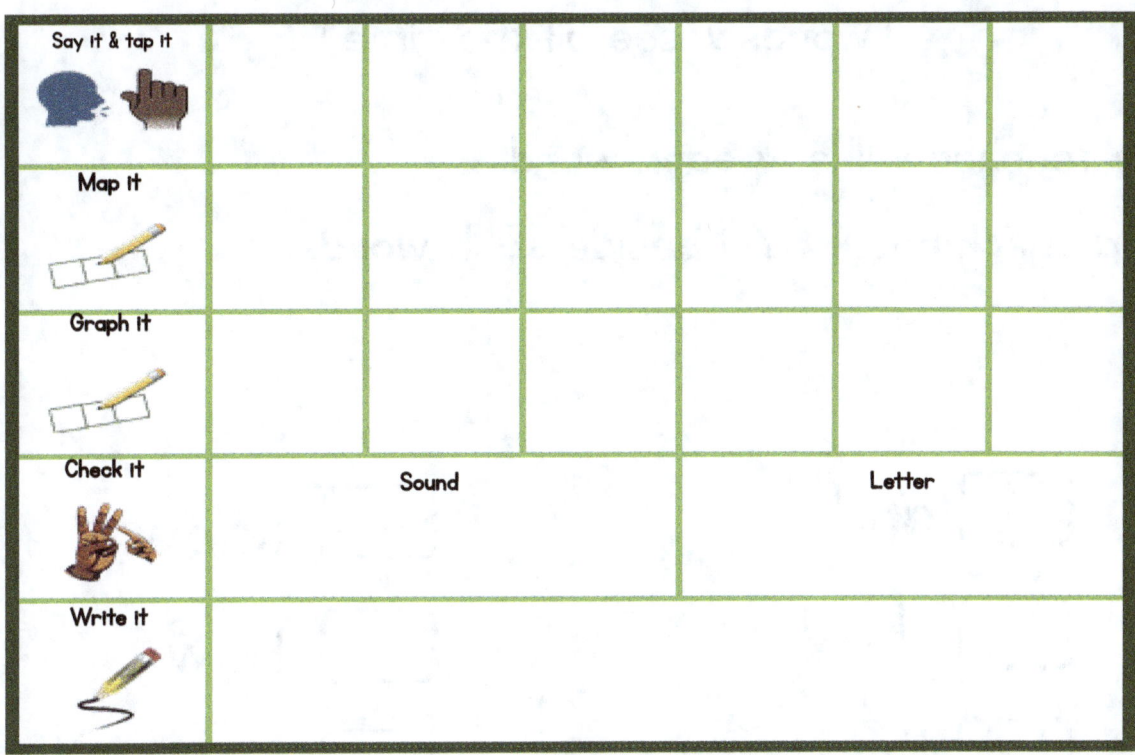

Say It & tap It					
Map It					
Graph It					
Check It	Sound			Letter	
Write It					

Say It & tap It					
Map It					
Graph It					
Check It	Sound			Letter	
Write It					

Put a ♥ above any part of the word that is tricky.

Get more words from C-DER® books 25, *At the Kite Festival;* book 26, *Time to Go;* book 27, *We Are Ready for Christmas;* and book 28, *Tam Gets in Trouble.* Use your poster to learn **-at** word families.

*Adapted and modified by CHEETAH® Toys & More, LLC for inclusion in this educational work.

188

Sight Words Activity

(words I see all the time)

Your teacher will say each word.

Put a check mark (✓) beside each word.

☐ and   ☐ know

☐ they   ☐ how

☐ from   ☐ said

☐ you   ☐ the

Sentences:

1. Cat can bake.

2. Kate has a kit.

I can read with you!

Name: _____

Cal and Kate
By Paul Law

Cal and Kate can bake a cake.
They got a kit from a sack on a rack.
"Do you know how to bake
a cake?" asked Cal.
"No, it looks hard," said Kate.
"Let us make a kite and not a cake.
A kite is the right pick," Cal said.

Answer these questions:

1. What did they want to make at first?

2. Why didn't Kate bake the cake?

3. What is the name of this story?

4. Who do you think drew the picture?

My Reading Record

Reading #1: ____ WCPM
Reading #2: ____ WCPM
Reading #3: ____ WCPM

Pupils take turns to use the iCHEETAH© microphone to call out words with and without the /k/ sound. Each time they hear or say a /k/ word, they lift one knee and balance on the other leg. Watch to see who correctly identifies the /k/ sound.

Read the C-DER® book, *At the Kite Festival.* After reading, make a paper kite and decorate the kite with /k/ sound words. Film your kite flying.

C is for crossing. With an adult, practise crossing the street.

Draw the letters *c* and *k* in chalk in your back yard.

Put the CHEETAH® sight words cards with a /k/ sound into a bag. Draw a card and read the word. If it has the letter *c*, march around the room. If it has the letter *k*, skip around the room.

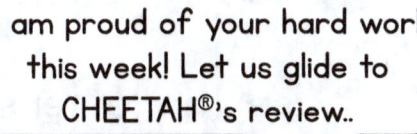

Colour the face that shows how you feel about the /k/ sound.

Got it!   **Almost got it**   **No, didn't get it**

I am proud of your hard work this week! Let us glide to CHEETAH®'s review..

Dear Parent: Date: _____

_____ does/does not fully understand the /k/ phonic sound. Please continue to review at home.

Signed: _____

Dear Teacher: Date: _____

Thank you. We have reviewed the /k/ phonic sound together. My child had a chance to teach me.

Signed: _____

Reward sticker for parent or guardian goes here.

Wonderful!

_____
(write name here)

Sticker for pupil goes here!

understands the phonic sound /k/.

CHEETAH® Review

Use the letters to make as many words as you can.

Circle all the words you make with the short ŏ sound.

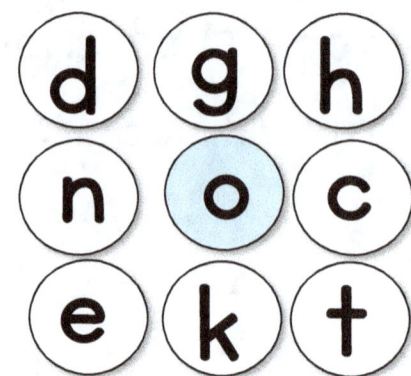

Solve the clues to complete the crossword.

Word bank

dig   stop

kite   head

help

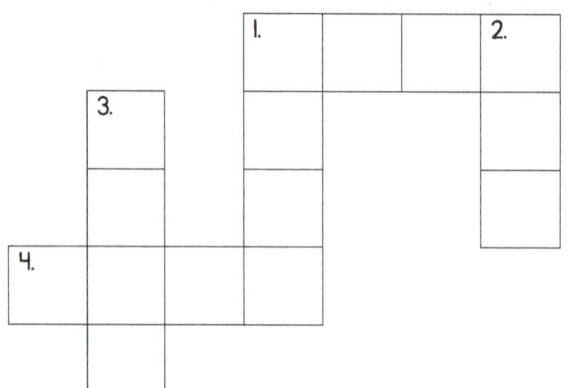

Across:
  1. The part of your body with eyes, ears, a mouth and a nose.
  4. Cars must do this when a traffic light is red.

Down:
  1. If you have a problem, you ask for this.
  2. You do this with a spade to make a hole.
  3. A toy you can fly on a windy day.

Let's create

Complete the table. Put the letters together to make words.

beginning sound	middle sound	end sound	words created
d g h c	o	t	dot, got, hot, cot
		g	
		p	
		k	
		w	

Use a different colour pencil crayon to draw circles around the words you do not know. Ask an adult what they mean.

Let's put together

Connect the boxes to make words from the -op word family. Write them in the given space.

h

m

-op   _____

p   _____

t   _____

_____

_____

Can you hear that the words in a word family all rhyme?

Let's take apart

Break each word into sounds. Write the letter that makes each sound.

Recognising phonemes will help you to read new words.

Let's trace

Trace the letters to write sentences.

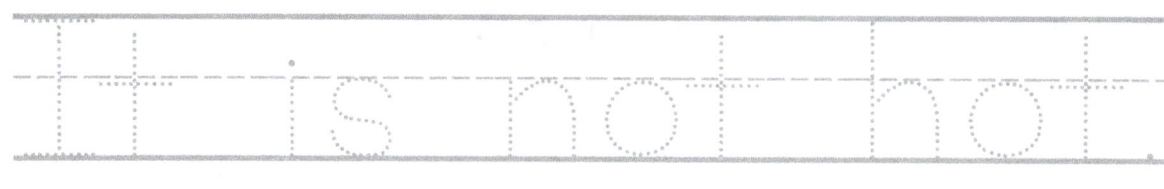

It is not hot.

A dog bit Sam.

Read the sentences you have written.

CHEETAH® Review

Look at each row. Circle the picture that has the sound at the beginning, middle or end of the word.

d	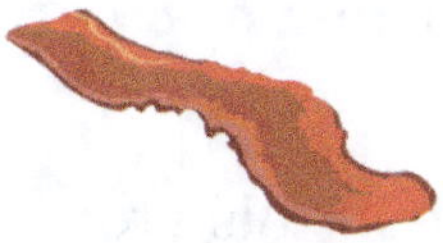		
short o			
hard g			
h			
hard c or k			

Find the Sight words in the wordsearch.

s	t	o	p	c
d	h	e	l	p
o	a	w	i	m
w	n	c	a	n
n	k	e	t	f

stop   down   help   thank   can

Set 3: Poster Story Fluency Test

NOTE: See the JamDER+ Poster Story for the story shown on the next page.

Sound and Letter Sets *: d, short o, hard g, h, c/k

Decodable words list:
Pam, Sam, Kit, a, sit, dock, on, it, deck, tan, not, get, sack, sock, rock, cop, in, get, top, and, kick, cat

NOTE: Not all these decodable words are in this story.

Sight words:
by, said, is, the, here, go, to, your, where, there, that

*As outlined by MOESYI

Fluency test instructions

On the next page, you will find the decodable reader presented as a fluency test. Fluent readers read effortlessly, recognising words automatically and gaining meaning from what they have read. By practising fluency, the child's ability to read with accuracy and expression will get better and better.

Step 1: Read the decodable reader for the first time and see how far the child gets in one minute. Quietly note how many mistakes are made and the final word they read before the minute is up. NOTE: do not stop the child if they make a mistake.

Step 2: Write the total number of words read on the words per minute (WPM) line.

Step 3: Write the total number of mistakes made on the mistakes per minute (MPM) line.

Step 4: Subtract the mistakes per minute (MPM) from the words per minute (WPM) to calculate the words correct per minute. Write this number on the words correct per minute (WCPM) line.

Step 5: Review the mistakes made together and have the child read the test two more times to practise.

Repeat this process every day for one week following the learning of the Set 3 sounds. Can you see the progress made?

Remember to use the additional resources such as CVC puzzles and flash cards.

Set 3: Fluency Test

Note: See this CHEETAH® Poster Story with images in the Pupil's Helper book.

Where Is the Sock?

Pam and Sam sit on the dock.	7
The cat is by the dock.	13
"Get your sock, Sam!"	17
"Is the sock in the sack, Sam?"	24
"It is not here, Pam!"	29
"Where is a cop, Sam?"	34
Pam and Sam go to get a cop.	42
The cop, Sam, and Pam hop to the dock.	51
"There it is! By the big red rock."	59
Pam and Sam kick the red rock.	66
"Kid, is that your cat?"	71
"Look! The sock!" said Sam and Pam.	78
She is a top cop!	83

Day 1	Day 2	Day 3	Day 4	Day 5
WPM: _____	WPM: _____	WPM: _____	WPM: _____	WPM: _____
MPM: _____	MPM: _____	MPM: _____	MPM: _____	MPM: _____
WCPM: _____	WCPM: _____	WCPM: _____	WCPM: _____	WCPM: _____

We all have chores; work to do. One of your chores is to learn to read. This takes time and you have to practise every day. Others, including me, will help you, but this is a chore that you have to do. One of your rewards is your ability to read and understand what you are reading. Come on, let's go! We have work to do.

CHEETAH® Reward Stickers

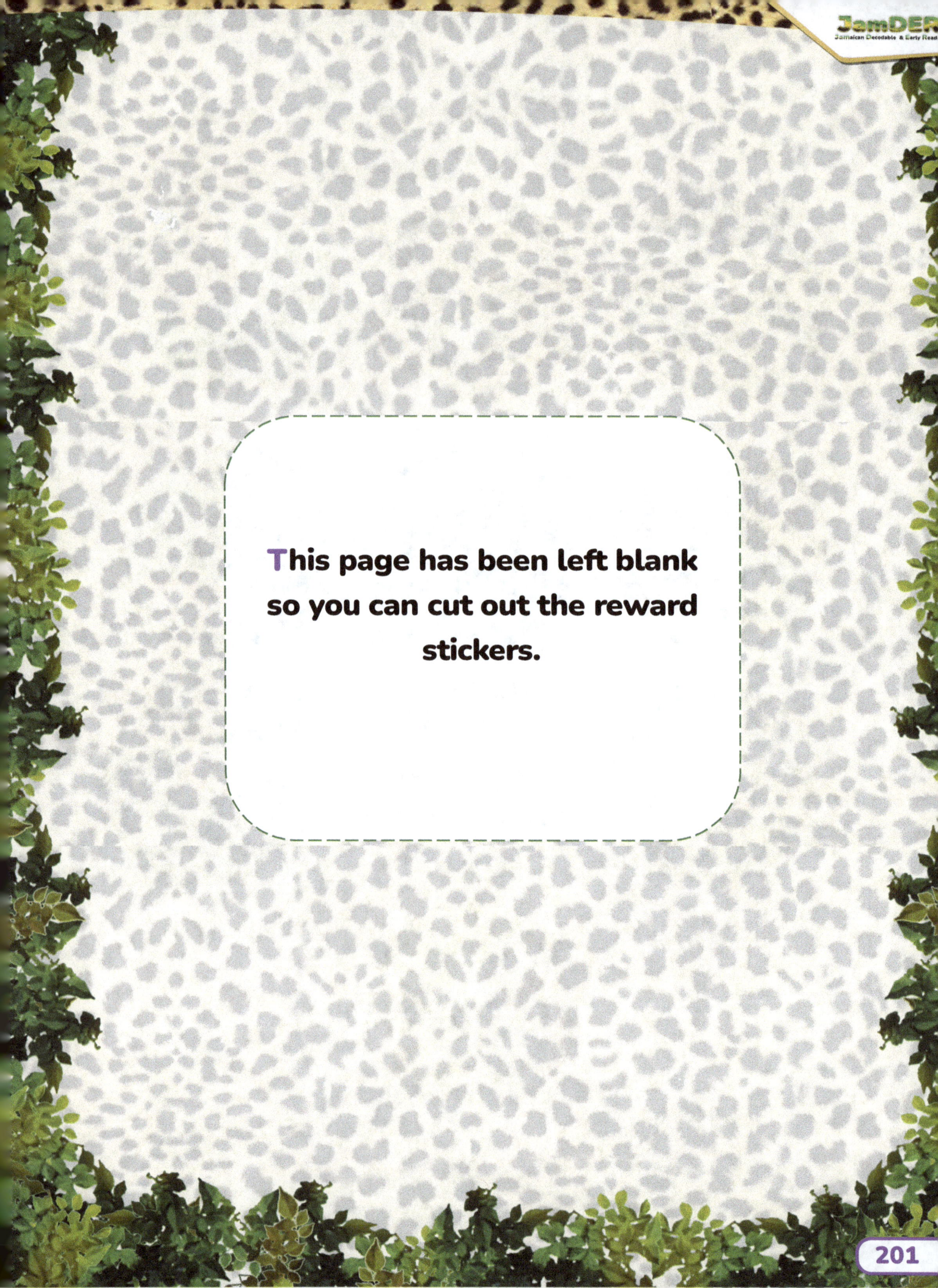

This page has been left blank so you can cut out the reward stickers.

Please refer to the corresponding CHEETAH® Poster Story Fluency Test for this set's focus sounds. Additionally, the following C-DER® books are recommended for comprehension and fluency practise:

Sound	C-DER® reference	Book title
l	Set 4, book 29	In the Sky
b	Set 2, book 14	Going Fishing
short ŭ	Set 4, book 34	A Bug on the Rug
soft g	Set 3, book 24	Hilda and Her Chicks
long ā	Set 4: book 37 book 55	Silly Willie The Big Race

Teaching tips*:

- /l/ – Voiced sound. Place the tip of your tongue lightly against the ridge just behind your top teeth (not pressing hard), let air flow around the sides of your tongue, and keep your voice on.
- /b/ – Voiced stop. Lips together, release a quick burst of air with voice and no added "uh" sound.
- short ŭ – Pronounced "uh" /ʌ/ as in cup. Jaw relaxed, tongue mid-central.
- soft /g/ – Pronounced /dʒ/ (as in gem). A voiced affricate that begins like /d/ and releases into /ʒ/.
- long ā – /eɪ/ as in cake. Start with the jaw slightly open, mid-front vowel, then glide into a smiling position.

Do you remember my name? What is your name? Do you know your mother's name? Not mommy, mamma, mum or mom. What is the name everyone else calls her?

Let us read book 29,
In the Sky.

CHEETAH® train loves a song, zooming as it hums along.
It whizzes through the land! Look! There's Lily in the sand.
Can you guess which sound is next?

Choose an instrument and let's make music together!

Lift your tongue tip to the roof of your mouth.

The /l/ sound is on the way to town.
The CHEETAH® train is slowing down.

203

The /l/ sound can appear at the start, in the middle or at the end of a word.

lion	**yellow**	**ball**
look	**please**	**will**
like	**old**	**tell**

Lily the Llama

My name is Lily, and I am a llama who lives on a hill. I have long yellow fur and black eyelashes. I love to play volleyball.

My friend Larry is lazy and never wants to play. He is a lion who likes to sleep. When he sleeps, his snoring is very loud! Larry's fur is also yellow, like mine.

I have other friends too, like Billy the lobster. But his claws are too big to play volleyball! The last time we played, he hit the ball so hard it landed in the lake!

Who are you? What do you like? Can you tell me about your friends too?

Listen to the word for each picture. Circle the picture that starts with the /l/ sound.

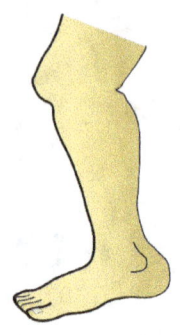

Practise writing the letter l.

Tip of tongue up behind top teeth, voice on. Excellent!

Listen to the story. Circle the letter L or l if you hear the /l/ sound.

Lola the Ladybug

Lola the ladybug loved to fly from leaf to leaf.

She lived on a large, green plant.

Lola liked to look at the world from high above.

Life was always lively for Lola.

/l/ sound = _____

My Word Wall

(from the story *Das at the Dam*)

Lib	lion	Leo	hill
	bell	had	little
went	up	have	am
big	as	lip	on

Colour the words you know.
You learn, leap, and lead!

My Word Work Mats*

Say & tap · Map (sounds) · Graph (letters) · Check · Write it

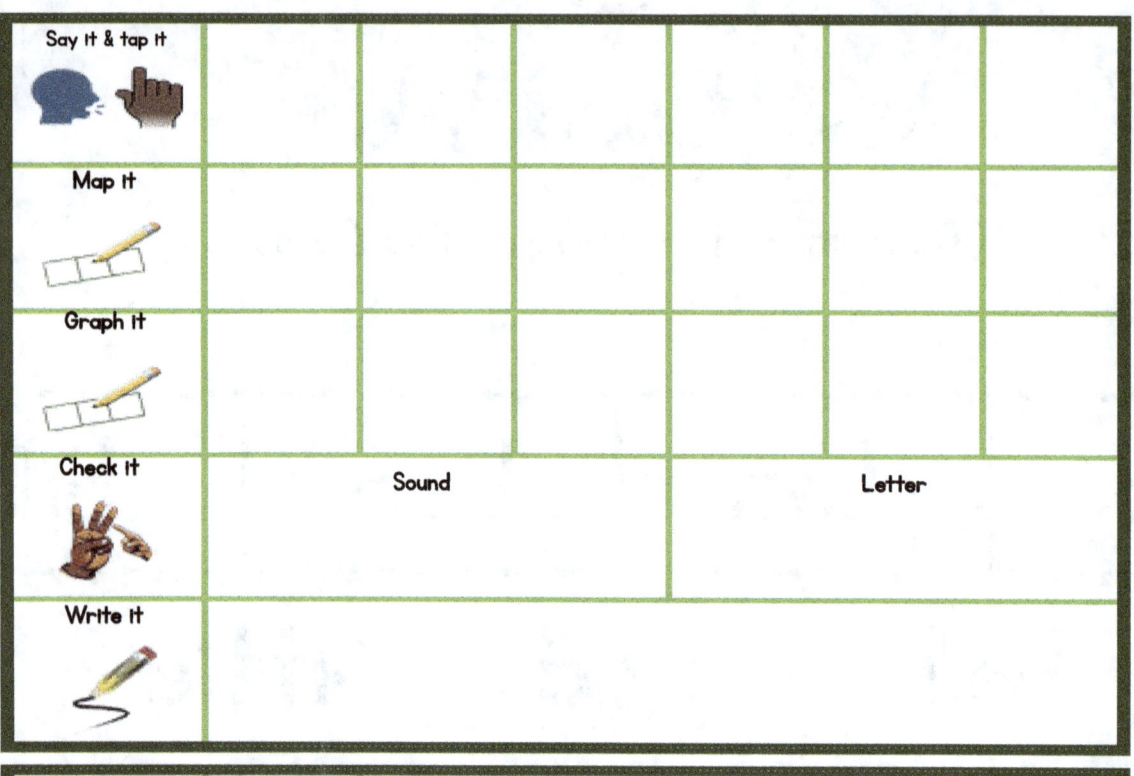

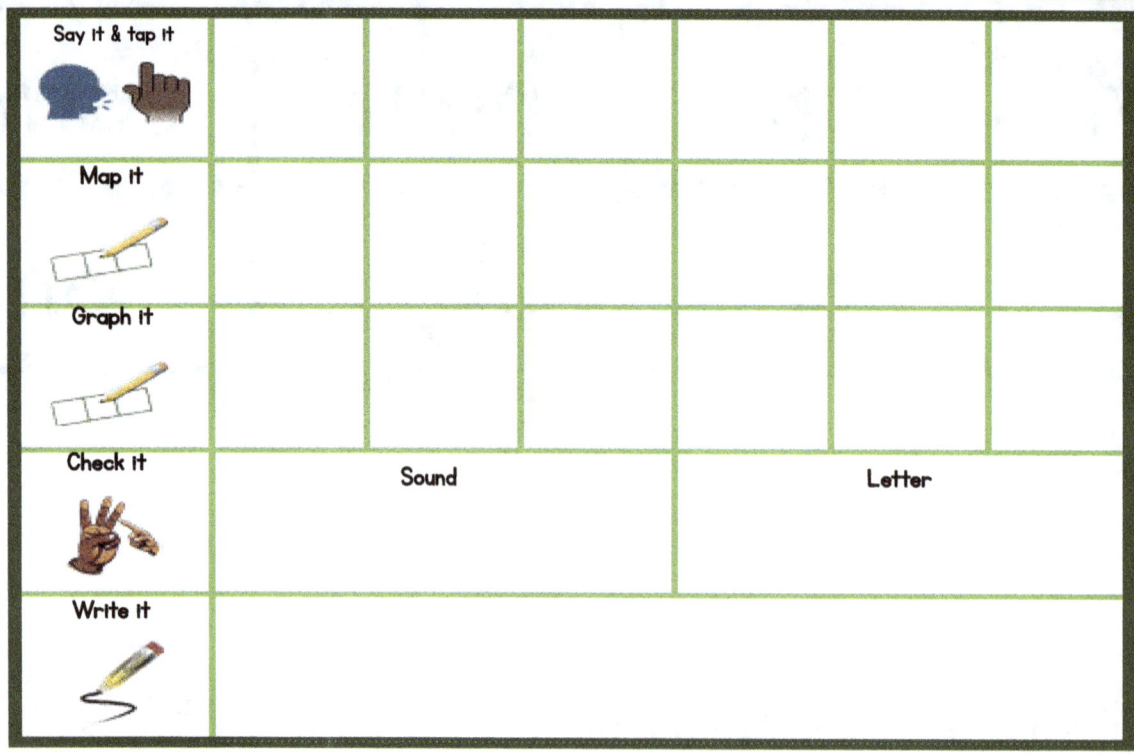

Get more words from C-DER® book 29, *In the Sky*. Use your poster (tool section in Volume 1) to learn the **-ib** word family.

*Adapted and modified by CHEETAH® Toys & More, LLC for inclusion in this educational work.

Sight Words Activity

(words I see all the time)

Remember the Cheetah® Chant©!

had _____

little _____

went _____

up _____

have _____

big _____

as _____

the_____

am _____

on_____

Sentences:

1. I went up the hill.

2. Leo is a big cat.

I can read with you!

Name: _____

Lib and the Little Lion

Lib had a little lion. His name was Leo. Leo was as big as a cat. Lib went up the hill. Leo went too. On the hill was a log and a bell. "Look, little lion," said Lib. Leo hit the bell. Leo and Lib had fun.

Answer these questions:

1. Who is Lib?

2. Where did Lib and Leo go?

3. Do you think Leo loves Lib? Why?

My Reading Record

Reading #1: ____ WCPM
Reading #2: ____ WCPM
Reading #3: ____ WCPM

Practise: /l/

Use the iCHEETAH© to tell you about the lion. As you listen, think of one fact you like best about the lion.

Look for objects with the /l/ sound. Make a display of them and write their names on labels.

Reread the C-DER® book, *In the Sky*. List the words with the /l/ sound. Focus on the word "*call*" and make other -all family words using the CHEETAH® letters.

L is for leg. Stand beside a friend and gently tie your inside legs together. Use a digital timer to time yourselves moving from one point to another. Can you better your time?

Paint animals with the /l/ sound, like lion, fly and owl. Where in their names is the /l/ sound?

Evaluate: /l/

Colour the face that shows how you feel about the /l/ sound.

Spead your wings and we will fly to the next sound!

Got it!

Almost got it

No, didn't get it

Dear Parent: Date: _____

_____ does/does not fully understand the phonic sound /l/. Please continue to review at home.

Signed: _____

Dear Teacher: Date: _____

Thank you. We have reviewed the phonic sound /l/ together. My child had a chance to teach me.

Signed: _____

Reward sticker for parent or guardian goes here.

Excellent!

_____
(write name here)

understands the phonic sound /l/.

Sticker for pupil goes here!

The /b/ sound

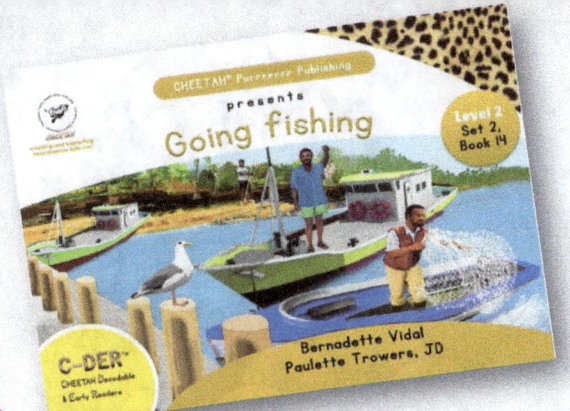

Let us read book 14,

Going Fishing.

CHEETAH® train loves a song, zooming as it hums along.
It speeds by in a rush! Look! There's Bobby with his bus.
Can you guess which sound is next?

Clap a pattern with your hands as you sing along with the song!

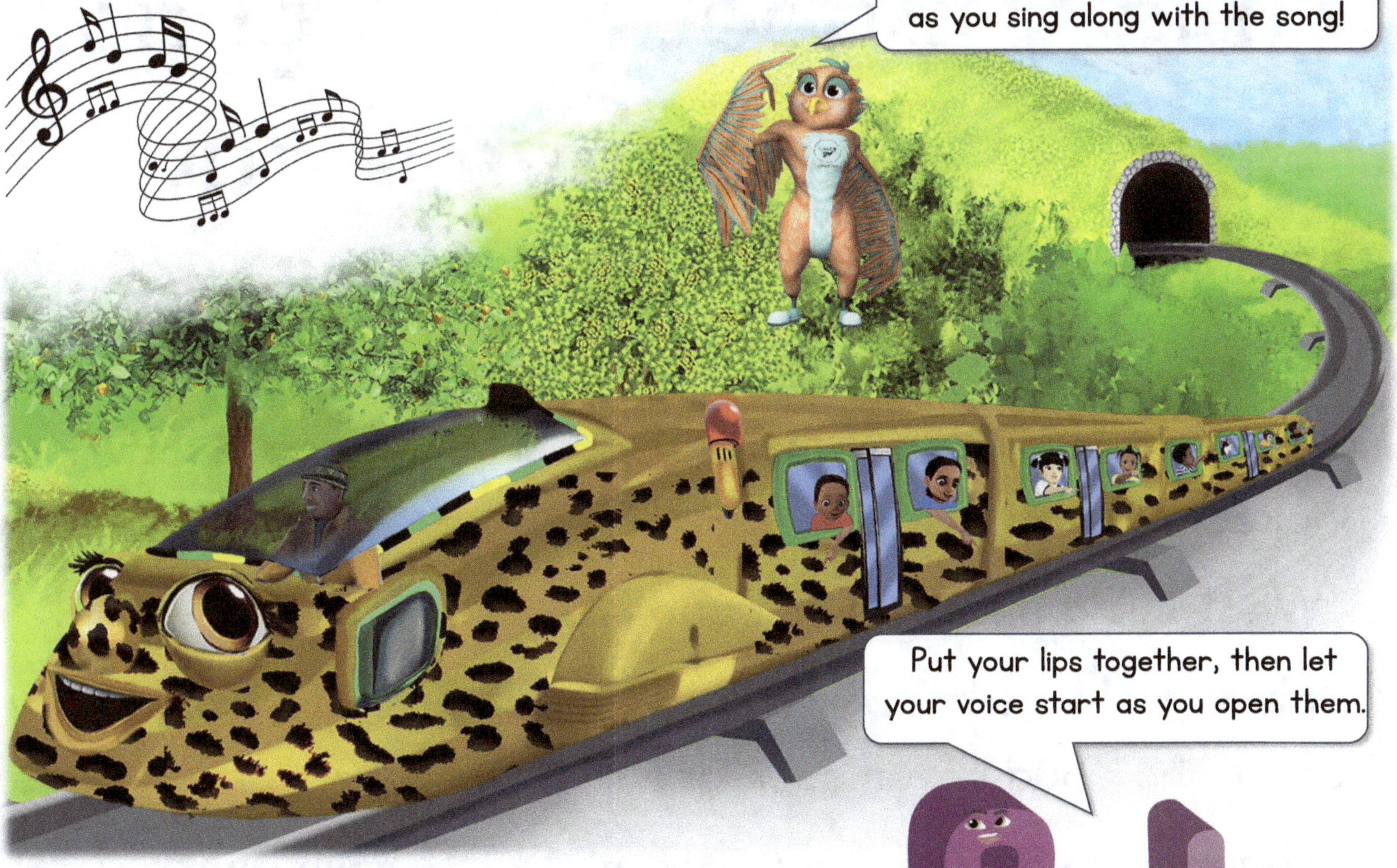

Put your lips together, then let your voice start as you open them.

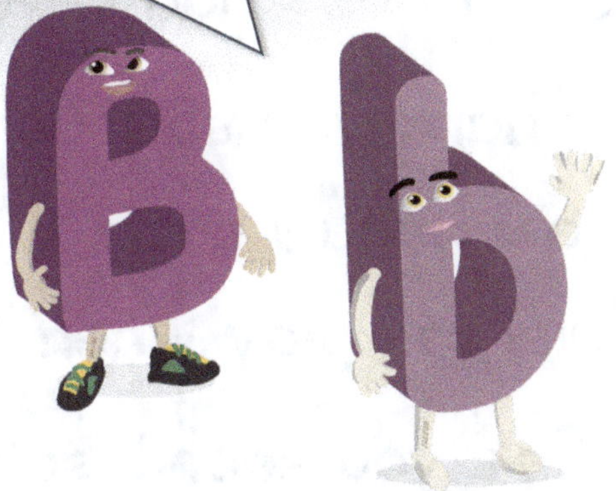

The /b/ sound is on the way to town.
The CHEETAH® train is slowing down.

Concept: phonic sound /b/

Bb

The /b/ sound can appear at the start, in the middle or at the end of a word.

blue

big

but

robot

about

goodbye

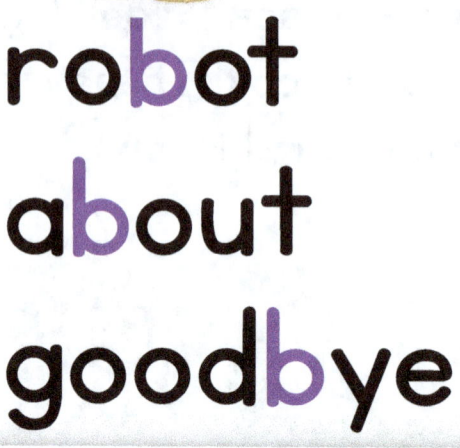

crab

grab

rub

Bobby has a Birthday

Yesterday was Bobby's birthday! His best friend Brian brought a big brown paper bag to his bedroom. Bobby looked inside and saw a black box.

"What could it be?" said Bobby.

Bobby grabbed the box and opened it. Inside was a toy bus. Bobby had never seen one like it before.

"Thank you so much," said Bobby. "But I have got to go now because my Aunt Ruby has baked me a big blue cake! We can play when I come back."

"See you soon," said Brian. They both waved goodbye. Bobby smiled. This was the best birthday ever!

pply: /b/

Listen to the words. Where do you hear the /b/ sound at the start, middle or end? Tell your teacher.

Practise writing the letter *b*.

Lips together, pop open with voice. Brilliant!

Listen to the story. <u>Underline</u> the letter B or b if you hear the /b/ sound.

Brave Billy

Billy had a book about a brave bear.

He would read it before bed every night.

"Bears are so big and brave," Billy would say.

Billy wanted to be as brave as the bear.

/b/ sound = _____

214

My Word Wall

(from the story *Ben and the Bag*)

Ben	big	bag	bed
	bug	bat	back
what	is	this	out
	said	his	

Colour the words you know.
Do your best every day!

My Word Work Mats*

Say & tap · Map (sounds) · Graph (letters) · Check · Write it

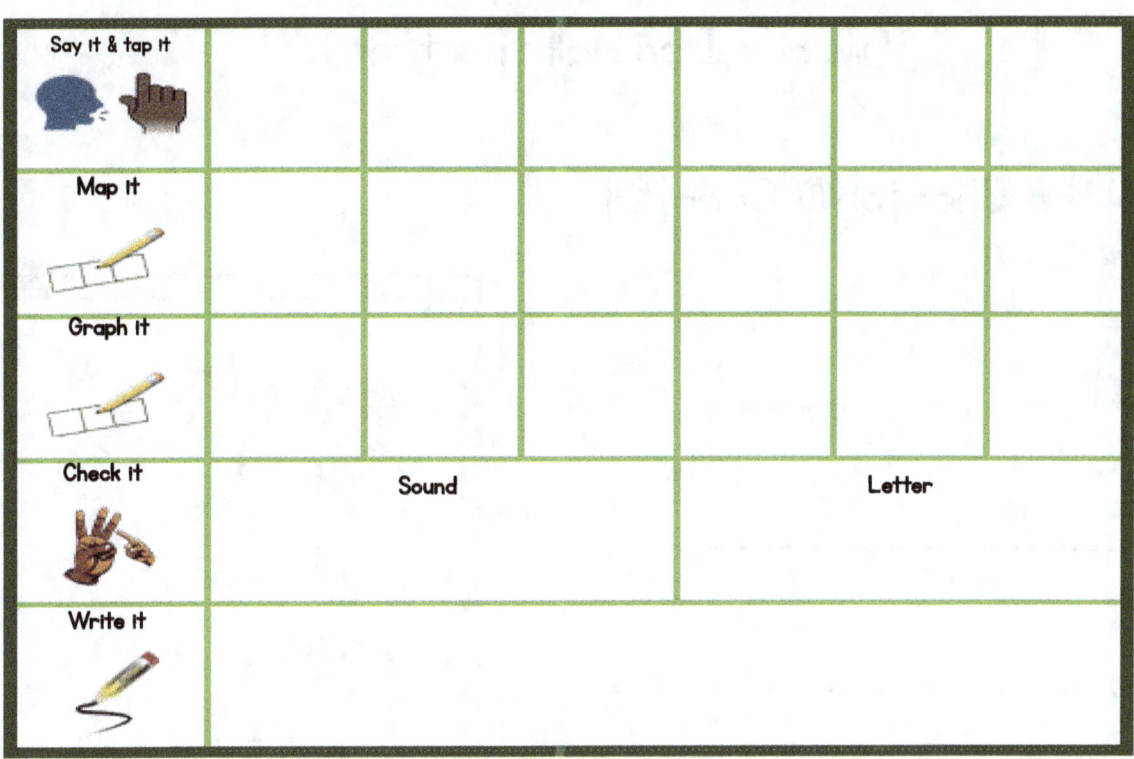

Bb

Say It & tap It					
Map It					
Graph It					
Check It	Sound			Letter	
Write It					

Say It & tap It					
Map It					
Graph It					
Check It	Sound			Letter	
Write It					

Put a ♥ above any part of the word that is tricky.

Get more words from C–DER® book 14, *Going Fishing.* Learn about the **-ed**, **-et**, **-en**, and **-ot** word families. Add the letter b to make new words.

*Adapted and modified by CHEETAH® Toys & More, LLC for inclusion in this educational work.

Sight Words Activity

(words I see all the time)

Do the Cheetah® Chant©!

what _____

is _____

this _____

out _____

said _____

CHEETAH®
Chant

1. 👂 Hear it
2. 👁 See it
3. 👄 Say it
4. ✏ Write it
5. 📖 Read it
6. 💡 Understand it
7. 🧑 Share it

Sentences:

1. This is Ben.
2. Ben had a bag.
3. The bag is big.

I can read with you!

Bb

Name: _____

Ben and the Bag

Ben had a big bag on the bed.
A bug got in the bag. Then
a bat got in the bag.
The bug bit the bag.
"Oh, no! What is in my bag?"
Ben got the bug out.
Ben got the bat out.
"Bad bug! Bad bat!" said Ben.
Ben had his big bag back.

Circle True or False for each statement.

1. A bug and a bat both got into Ben's bag. (**True / False**)

2. Ben kept the bug and the bat in his bag. (**True / False**)

3. Ben's bag was safe again because he got them out.
(**True / False**)

My Reading Record

Reading #1: ____ WCPM
Reading #2: ____ WCPM
Reading #3: ____ WCPM

Practise: /b/

Ask the iCHEETAH© to play the story about *Jack and the Beanstalk.* After listening, ask, "What are beans?" and "What do you think about Jack?"

Take turns with a friend to throw balls into buckets. Score one point if the ball goes in, and a bonus point if you can say a word with the /b/ sound.

Reread the C–DER® book, *Going Fishing.* As you read, look for words with the /b/ sound and write them in a word bank.

In a group, take turns to pretend you are something beginning with a /b/ sound, for example a bee, a bear, a ballerina or a baseball player. Can the group guess what you are?

Ask the iCHEETAH© to "tell me about Jamaica's birds." After listening, name one bird you heard about and share one thing you learnt.

Use fruits with the /b/ sound to make a fruit salad.

valuate: /b/

Colour the face that shows how you feel about the /b/ sound.

Remember, even owls have to learn before they can fly.

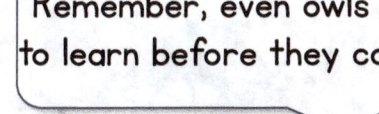

Got it!

Almost got it

No, didn't get it

Dear Parent: Date: _____

_____ does/does not fully understand the phonic sound /b/. Please continue to review at home.

Signed: _____

Dear Teacher: Date: _____

Thank you. We have reviewed the phonic sound /b/ together. My child had a chance to teach me.

Signed: _____

Reward sticker for parent or guardian goes here.

Brilliant!

_____
(write name here)

understands the phonic sound /b/.

Sticker for pupil goes here!

The short ŭ sound

Let us read book 34, *A Bug on the Rug*.

CHEETAH® train loves a song, zooming as it hums along.
It rushes up the hill, where bunny sits so calm and still.
Can you guess which sound is next?

Tap, shake, or clap and join the singing fun!

Your mouth is open and relaxed for my sound.

The short ŭ sound is on the way to town.
The CHEETAH® train is slowing down.

Concept: phonic sound short ŭ

The short ŭ sound can appear at the start or in the middle of a word.

umbrella

run

us

jump

under

funny

Bunny and the Sun

"Jump!" said the bunny to the puppy. "Jump and punch the sky!"

"Wow!" said the puppy. "Can you jump over the sun?"

"Maybe," said the bunny, and jumped higher than she had ever jumped before.

"Well?" she said. "Did I jump over the sun?"

"Not quite," said the puppy. "You were just under it!"

Then they heard thunder, and both the puppy and the bunny looked up to the sky. The bunny hopped upon a log and said, "Let us run home for a cup of tea before it rains." And off they went, under the clouds.

Apply: short ŭ

Say the name for each picture. Which picture starts with the short ŭ sound?

Practise writing the letter *u*.

Relaxed mouth, small open space, say ŭ like in up.

Superb!

Listen to the story. Circle the letter U or u if you hear the short ŭ sound.

Bud the Pup

A funny pup named Bud loved to run.

He would run up the hill and then run down.

"Bud, you run so much!" his mum would say.

But Bud found it so fun to run under the sun.

short ŭ sound = _____

My Word Wall

(from the story *Das at the Dam*)

sort
Uŭ

under	up	us	rug

pup	was	from

yes	let	get	of

on	out	cup	said

Colour the words you know.

You are unstoppable!

My Word Work Mats*

Say & tap · Map (sounds) · Graph (letters) · Check · Write it

sort Uŭ

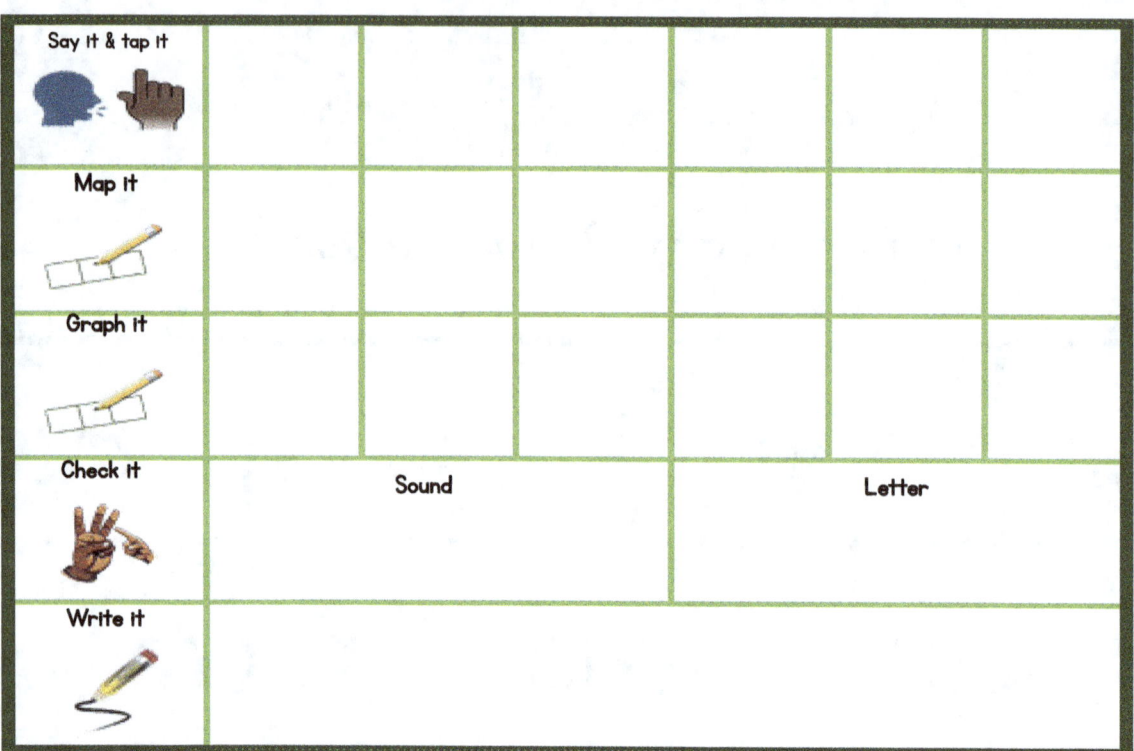

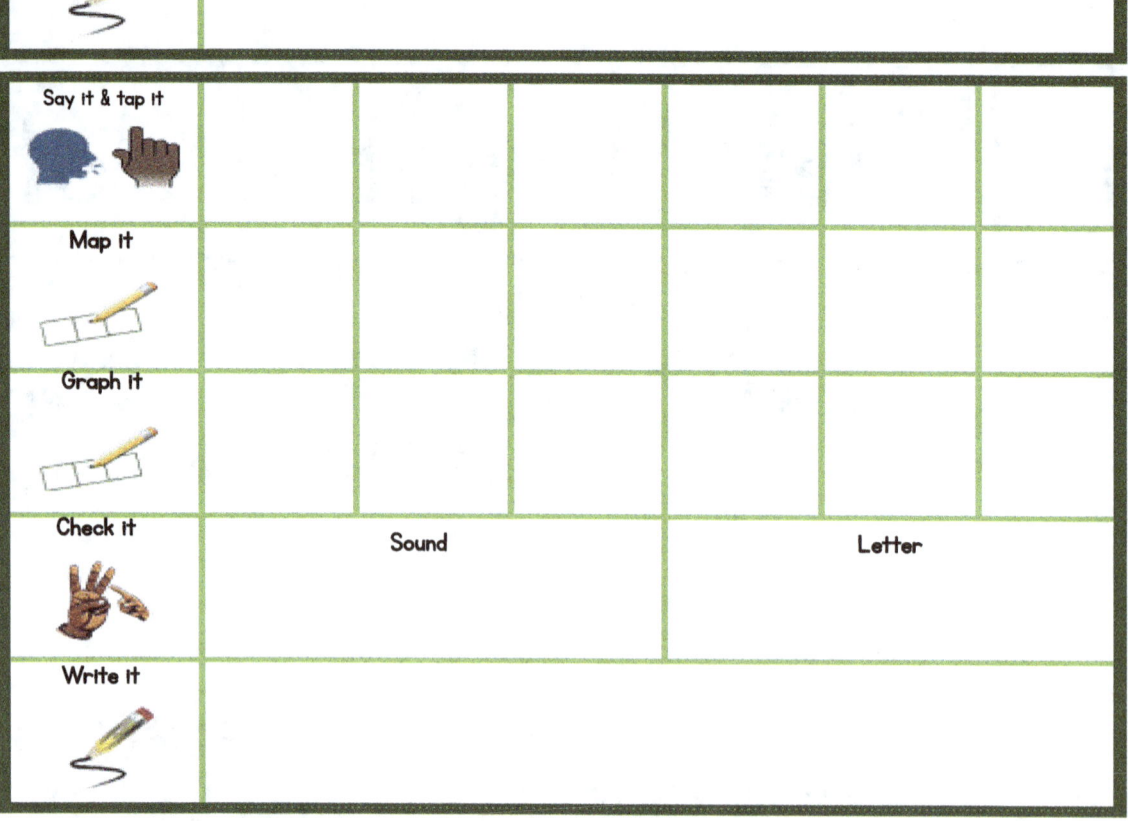

Put a 🧡 above any part of the word that is tricky.

Get more words from C-DER® book 34, A *Bug on the Rug*. Use your poster to learn the **-ug** word families.

*Adapted and modified by CHEETAH® Toys & More, LLC for inclusion in this educational work.

JamDER
Jamaican Decodable & Early Readers

Sight Words Activity

(words I see all the time)

Colour the words you know.
Ask for help with the ones you don't know yet.

was	from	under
yes	let	get
of	on	out
	said	

Sentences:

1. The sun was hot.

2. Get on the bus.

I can read with you!

Name: _____

Gus and the Pup

Gus the **cub** sat with Pop the **pup**. They sat under a rug.

The sun was hot over the rug. "Up, pup! Up! Let us get from under the rug," said Gus. "Yes, let us get out of the sun. Let us get on the bus," said Pop.

Answer these questions:

1. Where did the characters sit?
2. What is the opposite of under?
3. What is the meaning of cub and pup?
4. What do you do when it is too hot outside?

My Reading Record

Reading #1: ____ WCPM
Reading #2: ____ WCPM
Reading #3: ____ WCPM

Practise: short ŭ

Use the CHEETAH® Reading Partner© and the microphone in ChatGPT to record your reading of *Bud the Pup*. The Reading Partner will tell you how well you read.

Cut out an umbrella shape. Decorate the umbrella with the letter *u*.

Reread the C-DER® book, *A Bug on the Rug*. Use the CHEETAH® CVC puzzle pieces to make the short ŭ words you see in the story.

Think of more words in the -un word family.

With a group, place a selection of CHEETAH® sight word cards in a large outdoor area. Run to find all the short ŭ words as quickly as you can.

Use the -un words to write a poem together.

JamDE!

Colour the face that shows how you feel about the short ŭ sound.

The sky is the limit! Let us keep going together.

Got it!

Almost got it

No, didn't get it

Dear Parent: Date: _____

_____ does/does not fully understand the short ŭ sound. Please continue to review at home.

Signed: _____

Dear Teacher: Date: _____

Thank you. We have reviewed the phonic sound short ŭ together. My child had a chance to teach me.

Signed: _____

Reward sticker for parent or guardian goes here.

Super effort!

_____
(write name here)

understands the phonic sound short ŭ.

Sticker for pupil goes here!

The soft /g/ sound

Let us read book 24,
Hilda and Her Chicks.

CHEETAH® train loves a song, zooming as it hums along.
Gentle Geoff loves the train, riding home with his friend Jane.
Can you guess which sound is next?

Find a sound-maker and sing your heart out!

Can you make my sound 3 times?

The soft /g/ sound is on the way to town.
The CHEETAH® train is slowing down.

Concept: phonic sound soft /g/

G g

The soft *g* sound can appear at the start, in the middle or at the end of a word.

gem
gentle
giant

angel
danger
engine

cage
large
orange

Gill the Giant

Gentle Geoff the giant lived on the edge of a large cliff. He was so gigantic that nobody could speak to him because his huge head was so high up. On Christmas day, he heard a gentle voice behind him.

"My name is Gerry," said the voice. "I am a giraffe with an extra-long neck!"

Geoff turned around and came face to face with Gerry. Gerry wished him a happy Christmas and gave him an orange. "Thank you," smiled Geoff. "You have made this the best Christmas ever." The giraffe and the giant became the best of friends.

pply: soft /g/

Say the word for each picture. Circle the pictures with the soft /g/ sound.

Practise writing the letter *g*.

Lift the back of your tongue and voice it gently. Great!

Listen to the story. <u>Underline</u> the letter G or g if you hear the soft /g/ sound.

Gina Learns

At school, Gina loved to learn.

She learned about giant mountains and great oceans.

"Do you know about giraffes?" her friend Roger asked.

"Yes! They are gentle and tall, with a giant neck!"

/g/ sound = _____

My Word Wall

(from the story *Das at the Dam*)

soft
Gg

Gerry	gem	Gil	bag
	let	be	for
was	and	were	at
	had	from	

Colour the words you know.
You glow with greatness!

233

My Word Work Mats*

Say & tap · Map (sounds) · Graph (letters) · Check · Write it

soft
Gg

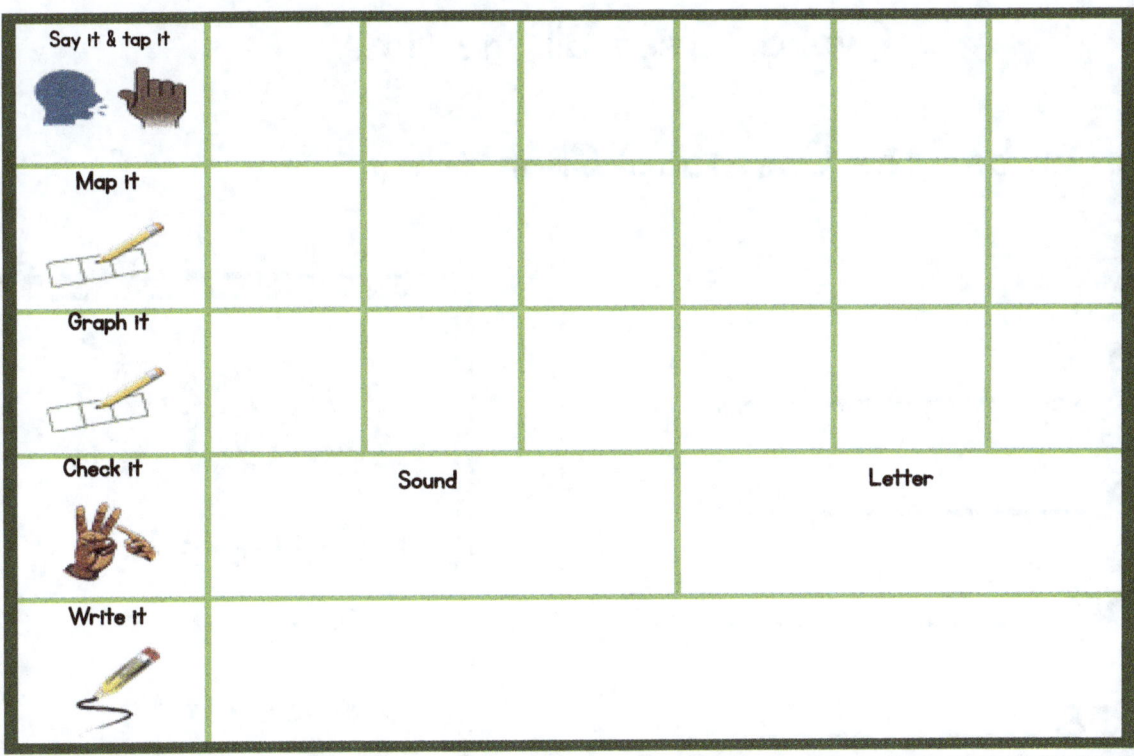

Say It & tap It

Map It

Graph It

Check It — Sound — Letter

Write It

Say It & tap It

Map It

Graph It

Check It — Sound — Letter

Write It

Put a ❤ above any part of the word that is tricky.

Get more words from C-DER® book *24, Hilda and Her Chicks.*
Add the letter **g** to the word families to make new words.

*Adapted and modified by CHEETAH® Toys & More, LLC for inclusion in this educational work.

Sight Words Activity

(words I see all the time)

Remember the Cheetah® Chant©!

let _____

be_____

for _____

was _____

and _____

were_____

had _____

from_____

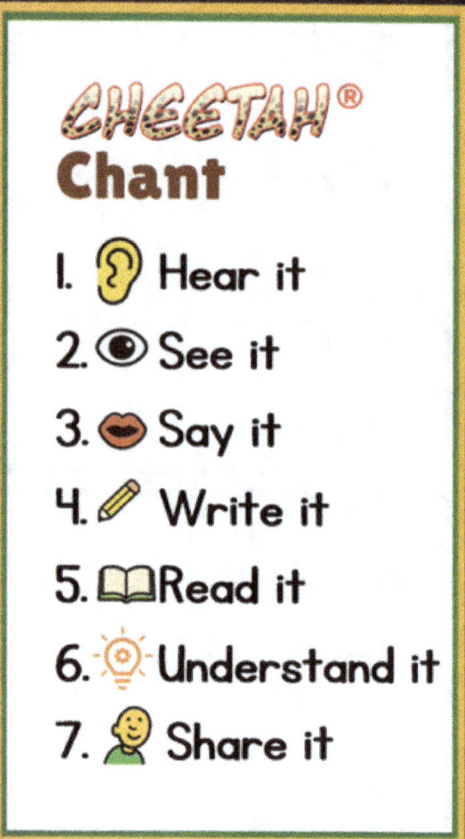

CHEETAH®
Chant

1. 👂 Hear it
2. 👁 See it
3. 👄 Say it
4. ✏️ Write it
5. 📖 Read it
6. 💡 Understand it
7. 🧑 Share it

Sentences:

1. I have a gem.

2. Let us sit.

I can read with you!

soft **Gg**

Name: _____

Gerry and the Gem

Gerry had a gem.
The gem sat in a bag.
Gil took the gem from the bag.
Gil said, "The gem is mine."
Gerry said, "No, the gem is mine."
"Let us sit," said Gerry.
"Let the gem be for us."
Gil put the gem back.
The gem was safe.
Gerry and Gil were pals.

Answer these questions:

1. Who said, "The gem is mine"?
2. How did Gerry and Gil solve their problem?
3. How would you feel if you had to share something special?

My Reading Record

Reading #1: ____ WCPM
Reading #2: ____ WCPM
Reading #3: ____ WCPM

Practise: soft /g/

With a friend, find soft /g/ words from a book or magazine and make a soft g word list.

Use the CHEETAH® Chart titled the *Two Sounds of* to explain how to tell the difference between the soft /g/ sound and the hard /g/ sound.

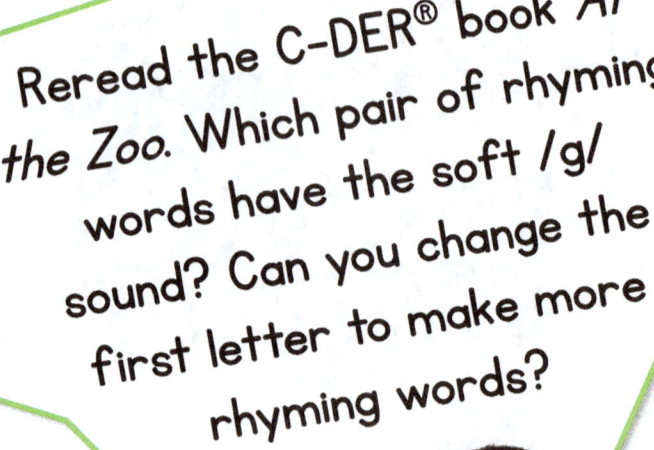

Reread the C-DER® book *At the Zoo*. Which pair of rhyming words have the soft /g/ sound? Can you change the first letter to make more rhyming words?

Use the CHEETAH® Reading Partner© to tes pupils' reading level using the CHEETAH® Poster Story, *Make a Game*. Thi test should be repeated at least two times.

Learn about germs and why it is important to wash your hands. Work with friends to make a video encouraging others to wash their hands.

Evaluate: soft /g/

Colour the face that shows how you feel about the soft /g/ sound.

Got it!   **Almost got it**   **No, didn't get it**

Believe in yourself, and you will fly high in your reading levels!

Dear Parent: Date: _____

_____ does/does not fully understand the phonic sound soft /g/. Please continue to review at home.

Signed: _____

Dear Teacher: Date:_____

Thank you. We have reviewed the soft /g/ phonic sound together. My child had a chance to teach me.

Signed: _____

Reward sticker for parent or guardian goes here.

Great job!

_____
(write name here)

understands the phonic sound soft /g/.

Sticker for pupil goes here!

Let us read books 37, *Silly Willie*, and 55, *The Big Race*.

CHEETAH® train loves a song, zooming as it hums along. Faye had baked a cake. She ate it as they passed a lake. Can you guess which sound is next?

Grab something noisy and sing loudly with us!

Start with your mouth open, then smile as you say my sound.

The long ā sound is on the way to town. The CHEETAH® train is slowing down.

Concept: phonic sound long ā

The **long ā** sound can appear at the start, in the middle or at the end of a word. It can be made with the letters a, *ay, ai, a_e*.

apron

ape

alien

baby

make

train

tray

may

play

Ray the Alien

Ray was a space alien. One Monday in May, he came to Earth to see his friend Faye. They ate cake and played games all day.

"Will you stay on Earth?" asked Faye.

"I am sorry, but I have to go away," said Ray, putting on a spacesuit that looked like a silver apron. "My mum says I have to make my bed and do my homework, but I will come back again tomorrow if I am able to."

Faye gave Ray a slice of cake. "Take this," she said. "And eat it when you are in space." She stayed and watched Ray's rocket fly away.

Apply: long ā

Say the names of all the pictures. Which pictures have the long ā sound? (Circle) them.

Practise writing the letters *a* and *e*.

Mouth open wide, tongue low – ā like in cake.

Listen to the story. (Circle) the letter A or a if you hear the long ā sound.

May's Cak

"May, your cake is amazing!" said Jay.

May had baked a cake that day.

"Thank you, Jay," said May.

"I found out how to bake from watching a play."

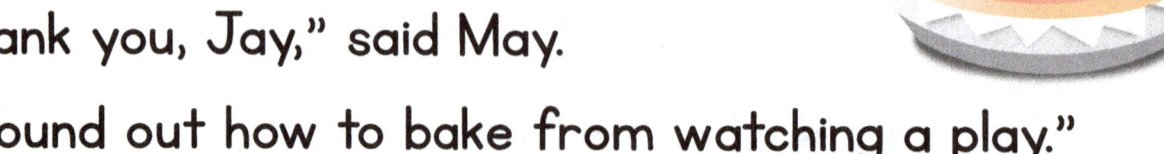

Long ā sound = _____

My Word Wall

(from the story *Das at the Dam*)

Fay	Ray	cake	make

rain	train	an

he	came	made	see

Colour the words you know.

Aim to be amazing every day!

My Word Work Mats*

Say & tap · Map (sounds) · Graph (letters) · Check · Write it

long
Aā

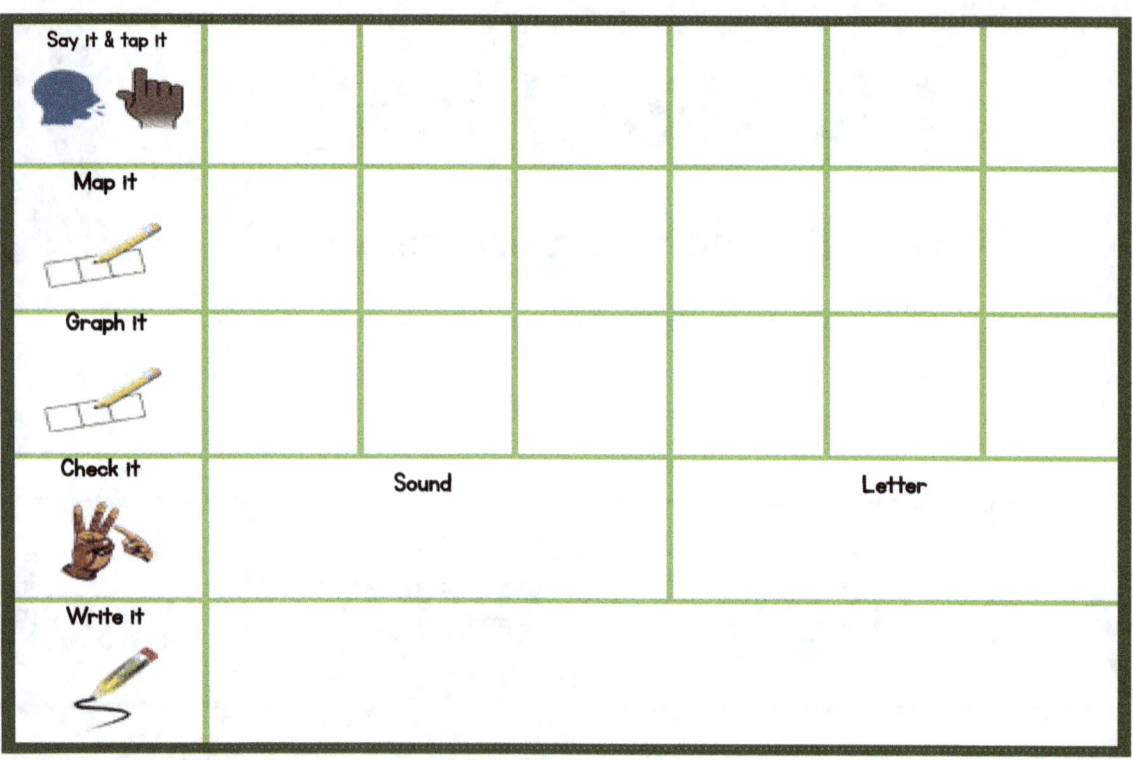

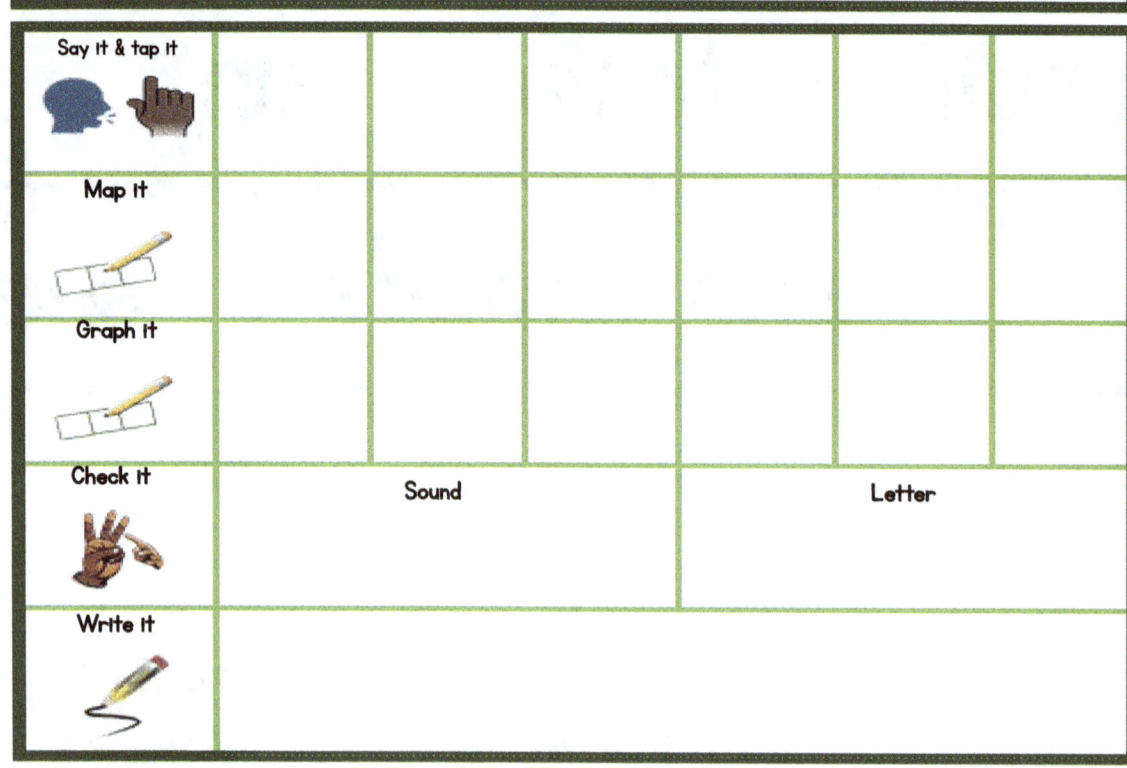

Put a 🧡 above any part of the word that is tricky.

Get more words from C-DER® book 37, *Silly Willie*, and 55, *The Big Race*. Use your poster to learn the **-ay** word family.

*Adapted and modified by CHEETAH® Toys & More, LLC for inclusion in this educational work.

Sight Words Activity

(words I see all the time)

Do the Cheetah® Chant©!

and _____

he _____

came _____

to _____

see _____

made _____

CHEETAH®
Chant

1. 👂 Hear it
2. 👁 See it
3. 👄 Say it
4. ✏️ Write it
5. 📖 Read it
6. 💡 Understand it
7. 🧑 Share it

Sentences:

1. Ray met Fay.

2. Fay made a cake.

I can read with you!

long
A ō

Name: _____

Ray and Fay

Ray was an ape.
He came to see Fay.
Fay made a cake for Ray.
They ate cake.
They played in the rain.
They went on a train.
Ray had to go.
"I have to make my bed," said Ray.

Answer these questions:

1. Who did Ray come to visit?

2. What did Ray and Fay do together?

3. Is this story real or make-believe?

4. What do you think will happen next?

My Reading Record

Reading #1: _____ WCPM
Reading #2: _____ WCPM
Reading #3: _____ WCPM

Practise: long ā

Make a paper plane and decorate it with the letter *a*. Measure how far it can fly.

With a friend, gather all the CHEETAH® sight words cards with the letter *a*. Sort them into long ā and short ă words.

Reread the C-DER® book, *The Big Race*. Look at the different ways the long /ā/ sound is made. Use the CHEETAH® letters to make words in the -a_e and -ai word families.

Write long /ā/ words on individual pieces of card, while a friend does the same. Muddle the words and use them to play a matching game together.

Use the iCHEETAH© with its microphone and karaoke mode to sing nursery rhymes. Listen carefully and repeat any long /ā/ sounds as you sing.

Set 4

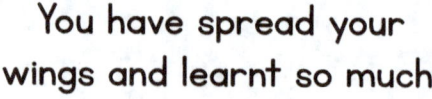

Colour the face that shows how you feel about the long ā sound.

Got it!

Almost got it

No, didn't get it

Dear Parent: Date: _____

_____ does/does not fully understand the phonic sound long ā. Please continue to review at home.

Signed: _____

Dear Teacher: Date: _____

Thank you. We have reviewed the phonic sound long ā together. My child had a chance to teach me.

Signed: _____

Reward sticker for parent or guardian goes here.

Amazing!

_____
(write name here)

understands the phonic sound long ā.

Sticker for pupil goes here!

247

CHEETAH® Review

Use the picture and the words to write a sentence. Don't forget to start with a capital letter and end with a period.

sun   is   big   The

is   blue   rug   The

baby   at   Look   the

Run   the   bus   to

Read the sentences you have written aloud.

Use the letters to make as many short ŭ and long ā words as you can. Letters can be used more than once, and nonsense words are welcome. Be creative and have fun!

CHEETAH® Review

Listen as an adult reads the blue words out loud. Find the words in the wordsearch.

blue but
say play
upon let
ate

b	u	t	p	s
l	u	m	d	a
u	p	l	a	y
e	o	e	t	r
i	n	t	e	n

Sound out the words you see in the pictures. Use the pictures to complete the crossword.

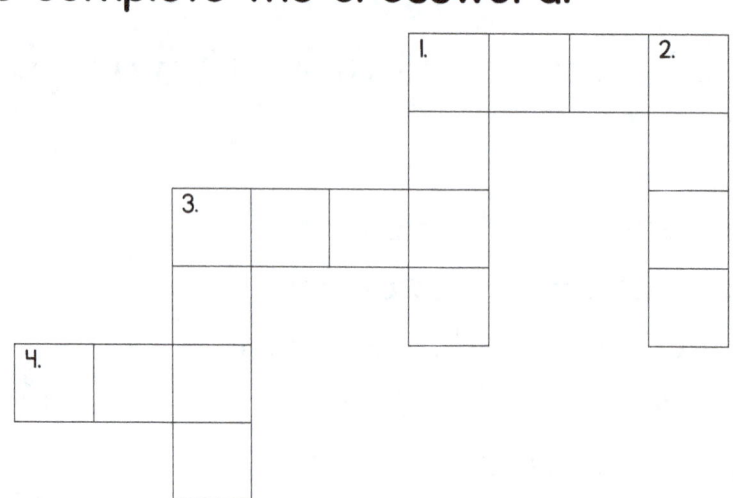

Across:
1.
3.
4.

Down:
1.
2.
3.

Let's create

Complete the table. Put the letters together to make words.

beginning sound	middle sound	end sound	words created
l b g	u a	t	
		g	
		m	
		n	

Sound out the words you have made.

List the words that you do not know the meaning of.

_____

_____

Read these words to an adult and ask what they mean.

Let's put together

Connect the boxes to make words from the *-ay* word family. Write them in the given space and read them aloud.

m

h

-ay

p

_____

_____

_____

_____

This word family shares the long a sound.

Let's take apart

Say what you see in each picture, then break each word into sounds. Write the letters that make each sound in the boxes.

bus

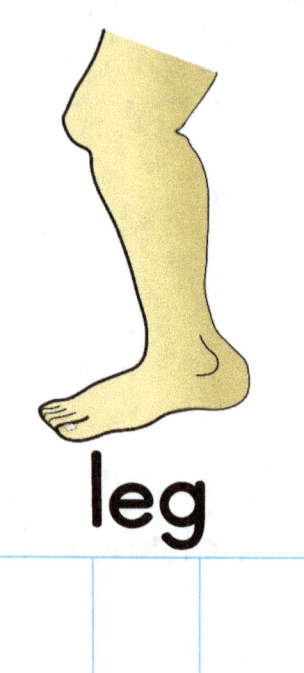

leg

crab

> Count how many sounds each word has.

Let's trace

Trace the letters to write sentences.

I am on the bus.

We fed the dog.

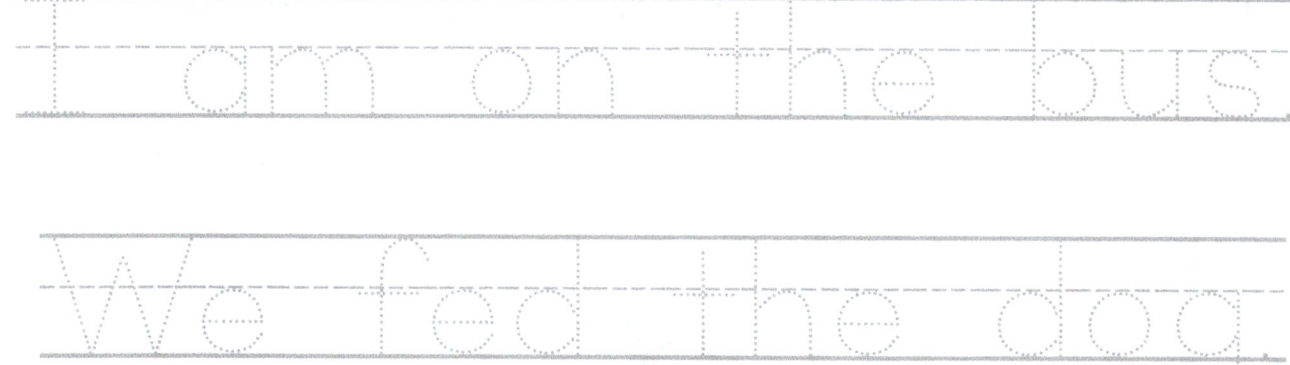

Read the sentences you have written out loud.

Set 4: Poster Story Fluency Test

NOTE: See the JamDER+ Poster Story for the story shown on the next page.

Sound and Letter Sets *: l, b, u, (soft) g, a (a-e)

Decodable words list:
Gus, late, Ben, lake, had, same, cape, sat, on, log, in, sun, made, cake, cat, came, name, Cal, gave, back, tug, fun, game, base, tape, ran, gem

NOTE: Not all of these words are used in the story.

Sight words:
was, to, the, and, a, he, see, of, his, one, with, two, by, good, said

*As outlined by MOESYI

Fluency test instructions

On the next page, you will find the decodable reader presented as a fluency test. Fluent readers read effortlessly, recognising words automatically and gaining meaning from what they have read. By practising fluency, the child's ability to read with accuracy and expression will get better and better.

Step 1: Read the decodable reader for the first time and see how far the child gets in one minute. Quietly note how many mistakes are made and the final word they read before the minute is up. NOTE: do not stop the child if they make a mistake.

Step 2: Write the total number of words read on the words per minute (WPM) line.

Step 3: Write the total number of mistakes made on the mistakes per minute (MPM) line.

Step 4: Subtract the mistakes per minute (MPM) from the words per minute (WPM) to calculate the words correct per minute. Write this number on the words correct per minute (WCPM) line.

Step 5: Review the mistakes made together and have the child's read the test two more times to practise.

Repeat this process every day for one week following the learning of the Set 4 sounds. Can you see the progress made?

> Remember to use the additional resources such as CVC puzzles and flash cards.

Set 4: Fluency Test

Note: See this CHEETAH® Poster Story with images in the Pupil's Helper book.

Make A Game

Gus was late to see Ben at the lake!	9
Ben and Gus had the same cape!	16
Gus and Ben sat on a log in the sun.	26
Ben made a cake. He gave some cake to Gus.	36
The cat came to see Ben.	42
The cat had a name tag with a gem.	51
Cal gave the back of the cape a tug.	60
Gus gave his cape to Cal.	66
Cal, Ben, and Gus made a fun game.	74
Gus made base one with tape.	80
Ben made base two by the lake.	87
Gus ran to the base with Cal.	94
"Good game, Gus and Cal!" said Ben.	101

Day 1	Day 2	Day 3	Day 4	Day 5
WPM: _____	WPM: _____	WPM: _____	WPM: _____	WPM: _____
MPM: _____	MPM: _____	MPM: _____	MPM: _____	MPM: _____
WCPM: _____	WCPM: _____	WCPM: _____	WCPM: _____	WCPM: _____

CHEETAH® Reward Stickers

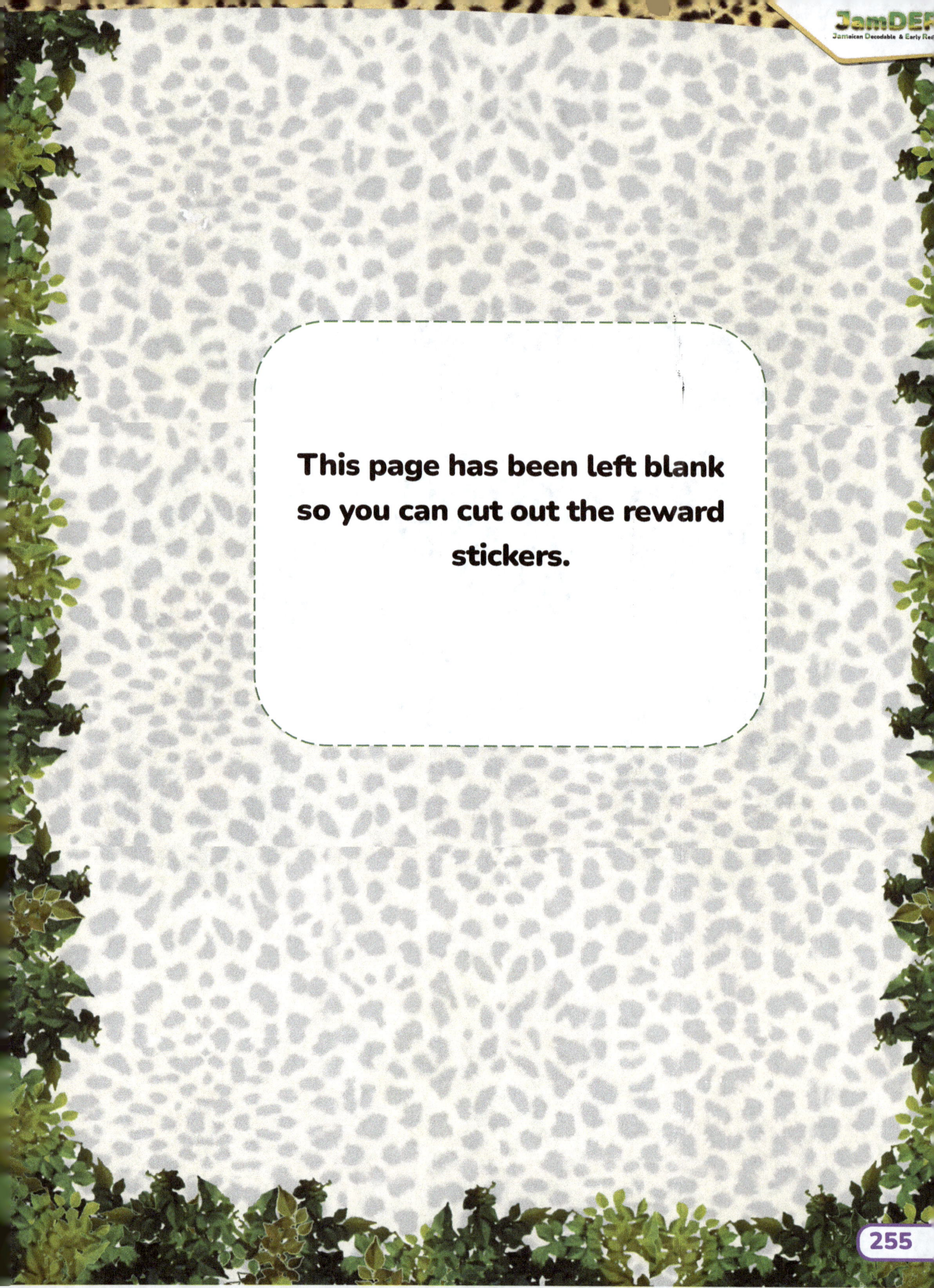

This page has been left blank so you can cut out the reward stickers.

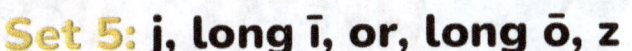

Set 5: j, long ī, or, long ō, z

Please refer to the corresponding CHEETAH® Poster Story Fluency Test for this set's focus sounds. Additionally, the following C-DER® books are recommended for comprehension and fluency practise:

Sound	C-DER® reference	Book title
j	Set 5, book 38	Visiting Aunt Jen and Uncle Joe
long ī	Set 5, book 39	Riding My Bike
or	Set 5, book 40	Gor Shore Adventure
long ō	Set 5, book 41	Sam's Boat
z	Set 5: book 42 book 43	Party Time! At the Zoo

Teaching tips*:

- /j/ – Voiced affricate /dʒ/ as in jam. Start with tongue tip at the alveolar ridge (like /d/) and release into /ʒ/ with voice.
- long ī – Diphthong /aɪ/ as in my. Start with mouth open and tongue low-front, then glide up toward high-front.
- /or/ – /ɔr/ as in or. Lips rounded, tongue mid-back moving toward /r/.
- long ō – Diphthong /oʊ/ as in go. Lips rounded mid-position, then glide toward a higher position, sometimes ending with a slight /w/ glide.
- /z/ – Voiced fricative. Teeth close together, tongue just behind top teeth, push air through a narrow space while using your voice so it buzzes: "zzzzzz."

Hi! Remember my name? I am here to guide you to the highest heights in reading. The sky is the limit. Let's soar together!

Let us read book 38, *Visiting Aunt Jen* and *Uncle Joe.*

CHEETAH® train loves a song, zooming as it hums along.
Uncle John loves a joke, laughing with the jolly folk.
Can you guess which sound is next?

Pick up an instrument and play along with the tune!

Watch in a mirror as you make my sound!

The /j/ sound is on the way to town.
The CHEETAH® train is slowing down.

Concept: phonic sound /j/

The /j/ sound can appear at the start or in the middle of a word. It is the same as a soft g.

jar

jump

just

enjoy

object

banjo

Janet and Jake

Janet and Jake are brother and sister. In January, they took a ride on a jumbo jet to see their family.

When they arrived, Uncle John was on the porch, laughing and playing his banjo. He loved to tell jokes. Mum and dad had just got home from work.

Mum took off her jacket and said, "Janet! Jake! You have come home to see us!" She jumped and danced with joy. "Come inside! I have made jelly for us all to enjoy!"

Janet and Jake smiled and went into the house. They love their family very much.

Apply: /j/

Listen to the words for each picture. Colour the pictures with the /j/ sound.

Practise writing the letter j.

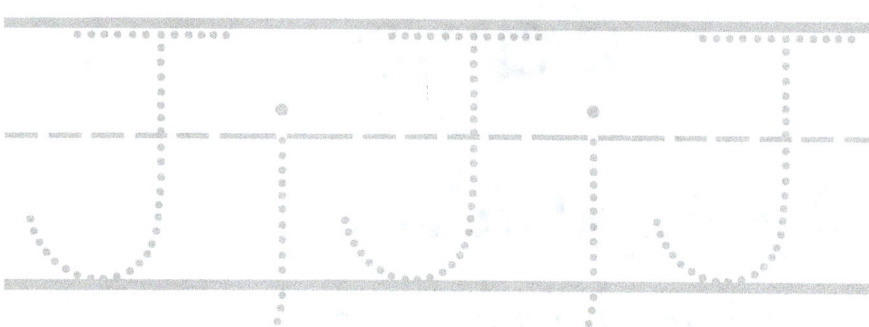

Lips out a little, tongue middle up, voice on.

Great job!

Listen to the story. (Circle) the letter J or j if you hear the /j/ sound.

Jolly Jen

Jen's family is big and jolly.

"I have three jolly brothers," she says.

We play and enjoy a joke together.

"With my family, every day is joyful," Jen says.

/j/ sound = _____

My Word Wall

(from the story Jake and Jamaica)

Jake	Jamaica	Jane	jam

jar	joy	jog

ask	that	make

you	jump

Colour the words you know.
Jump for joy! You are a reader!

260

My Word Work Mats*

Say & tap · Map (sounds) · Graph (letters) · Check · Write it

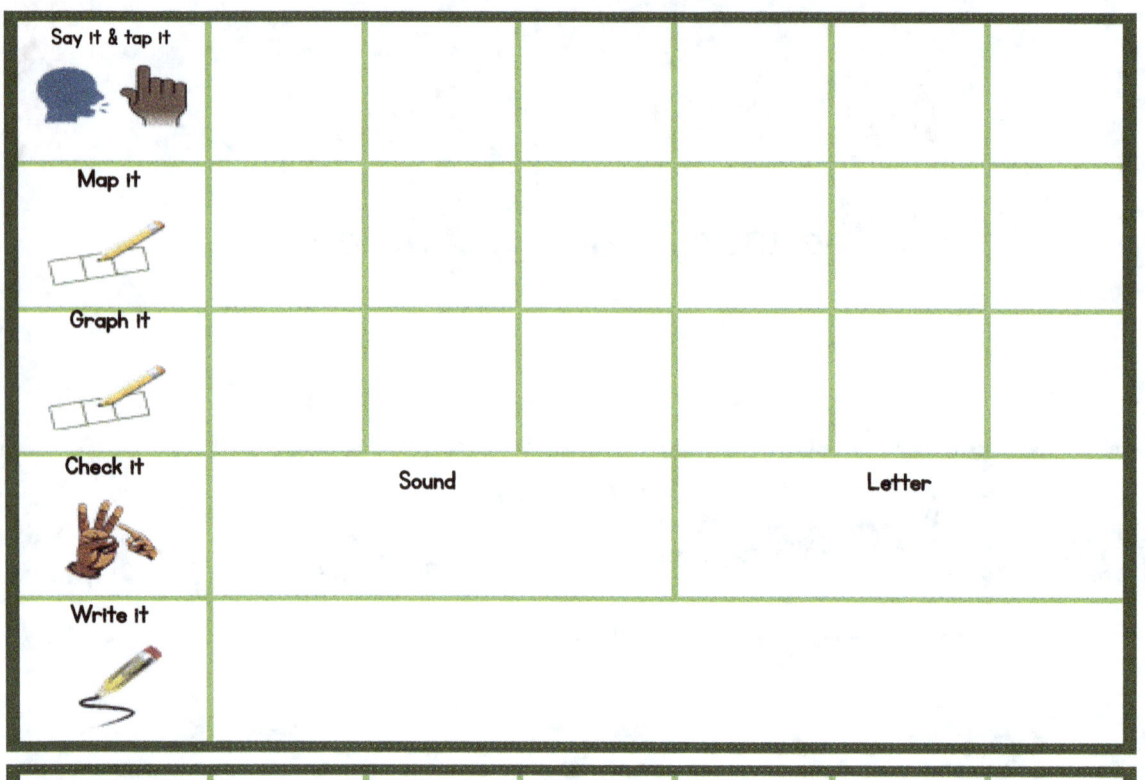

Say It & tap It						
Map It						
Graph It						
Check It	Sound			Letter		
Write It						

Say It & tap It						
Map It						
Graph It						
Check It	Sound			Letter		
Write It						

Put a ♥ above any part of the word that is tricky.

Get more words from C-DER® book 38, *Visiting Aunt Jen and Uncle Joe.* Count the number of times you see the letter **J** or **J**.

*Adapted and modified by CHEETAH® Toys & More, LLC for inclusion in this educational work.

Sight Words Activity

(words I see all the time)

Colour the words you know. Learn the ones you do not know yet. Remember the CHEETAH® Chant!

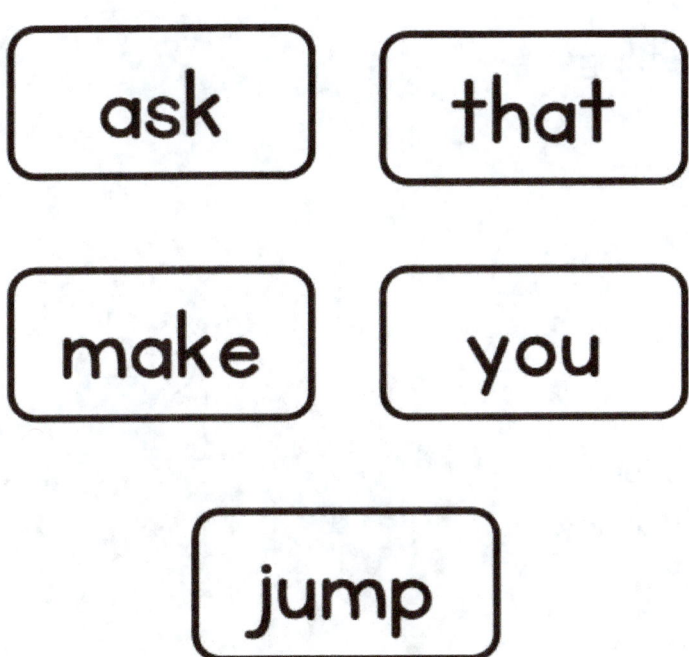

CHEETAH®
Chant

1. 👂 Hear it
2. 👁 See it
3. 👄 Say it
4. ✏ Write it
5. 📖 Read it
6. 💡 Understand it
7. 🧑 Share it

Sentences:

1. Can you jog?

2. I can jump!

I can read with you!

Name: _____

Jake and Jamaica

Jake loves Jamaica.
"Jamaica?" asked Jane.
"Is it a jam? Is it in a jar?
Is it a maker? Is it something
that makes you jump for joy?"
"Yes and no," said Jake.
"Jamaica is a gem!
It has jungle, jazz, and jerk
for your food.
You can jog on the sand,
jump in the sun,
and meet people who are jolly.
Jamaica makes me jump for joy.
I love Jamaica!"

Answer these questions:

1. What did Jake say Jamaica has?
2. How did Jake describe the people in Jamaica?
3. What is the story mostly about?

My Reading Record

Reading #1: ____ WCPM
Reading #2: ____ WCPM
Reading #3: ____ WCPM

Practise: /j/

Work with a friend. What things can you jump over? How far can you jump? Measure the distance.

Ask the iCHEETAH© to tell you about Jamaica. Listen so you can tell the class one interesting fact you learnt.

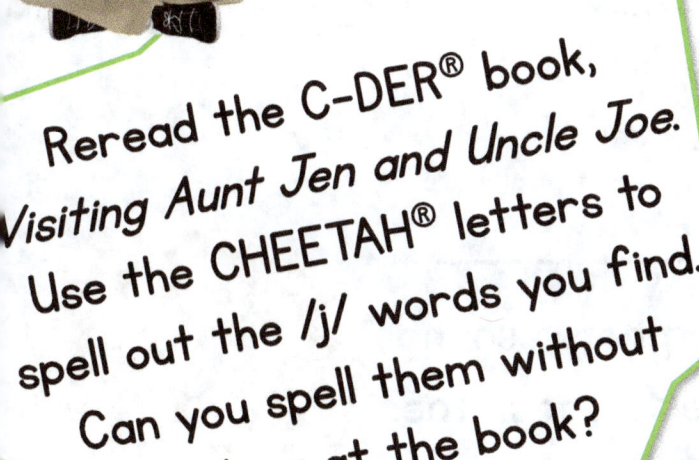

Reread the C-DER® book, *Visiting Aunt Jen and Uncle Joe.* Use the CHEETAH® letters to spell out the /j/ words you find. Can you spell them without looking at the book?

Working with a friend, how many /j/ CVC words can you make using the CHEETAH® letters?

Use a jug to fill different sized containers with water. Record how many jugs of water each container holds.

Draw the letter *J.* Cut it into pieces to create a jigsaw.

Set 5

Colour the face that shows how you feel about the /j/ sound.

You are growing all the time. Keep spreading your wings!

Got it!

Almost got it

No, didn't get it!

Dear Parent: Date: _____

_____ does/does not fully understand the phonic sound /j/. Please continue to review at home.

Signed: _____

Dear Teacher: Date: _____

Thank you. We have reviewed the phonic sound /j/ together. My child had a chance to teach me.

Signed: _____

Reward sticker for parent or guardian goes here.

Great job!

_____

(write name here)

Sticker for pupil goes here!

understands the phonic sound /j/.

Let us read book 39,
Riding My Bike.

CHEETAH® train loves a song, zooming as it hums along.
Mike is on his bike. He wants to fly his kite tonight.
Can you guess which sound is next?

Let's make music – find your instrument and sing along!

Can you make my sound 3 times?

The long Ī sound is on the way to town.
The CHEETAH® train is slowing down.

Concept: phonic sound long I 🔊

The long I sound can appear at the start, in the middle or at the end of a word. It can be made with the letters *i*, *ie*, igh, *i_e* or *y*.

ice

I

island

five

like

find

pie

my

high

Who is Mike?

My name is Mike. I am five years old. I like to ride my bike and fly my kite high in the sky. It is nice to ride my bike across the island, under the pine trees. When I stop for a rest, I fly my kite.

One day, I would like to paint my kite, maybe red like fire or white like ice. That way I will see it dancing when it is up in the sky.
And if it flies away, it will be easy to find.

My favourite food is pie. I like to eat chicken pie for dinner and apple pie for dessert.
What do you like to do? Do you like pie too?

Apply: /ī/

Listen to the word for each picture. Colour the pictures with the long ī sound.

Practise writing the letters *i* and *e*.

Start with your mouth open. Your lips move into a smile as the sound ends.

Listen to the story. Circle the letter I or i if you hear the long ī sound.

The Spider

Iris saw a spider under a pile of paper.

She cried, "Quick! Hide!"

"The spider is tiny!" Mike said. "I have an idea."

"I will hide him in my hands and take him outside."

Long ī sound = _____

My Word Wall

(some words from the story *Who Am I*)

I	ice	island	Mike

kite	bike	fly

ride	white	my	like

who	yellow	one

Colour the words you know.

Smile. You are doing great!

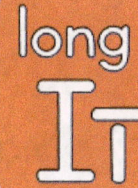

My Word Work Mats*

Say & tap · Map (sounds) · Graph (letters) · Check · Write it

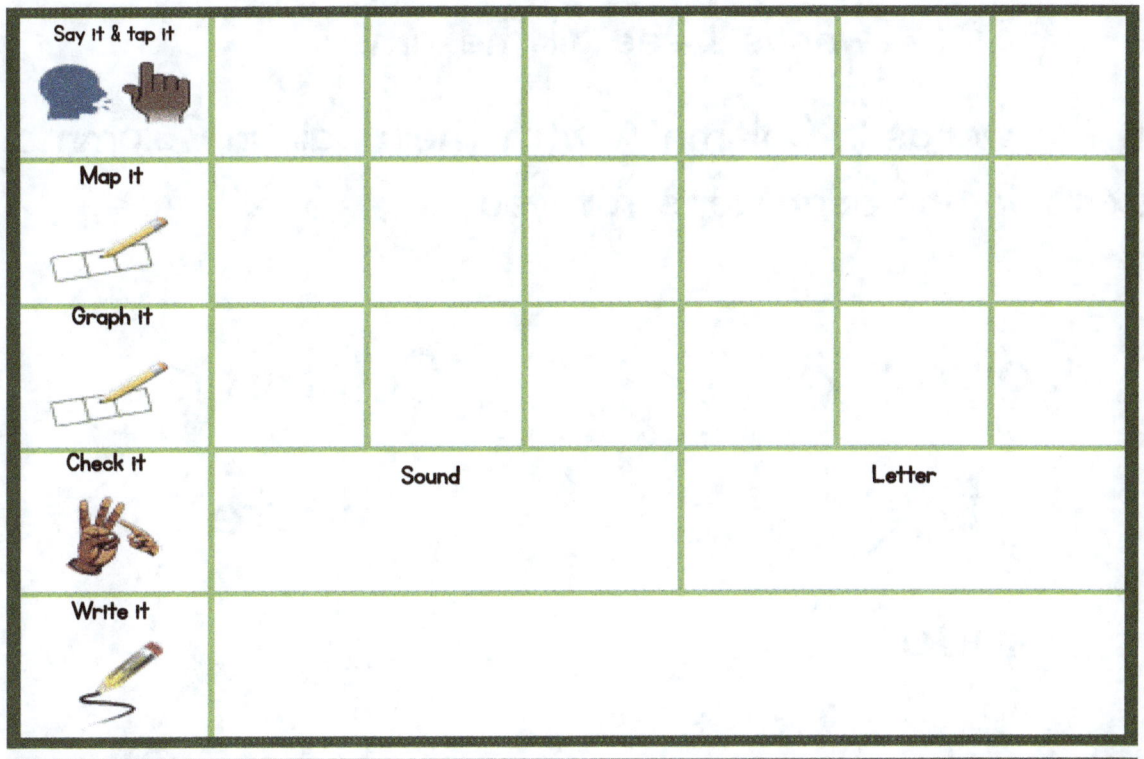

long

I T

Say it & tap it

Map it

Graph it

Check it | Sound | Letter

Write it

Put a ♥ above any part of the word that is tricky.

Get more words from book 39, *Riding My Bike*. Write the page numbers where you find the words ride, bike, and Mike in the story.

*Adapted and modified by CHEETAH® Toys & More, LLC for inclusion in this educational work.

Sight Words Activity

(words I see all the time)

Match the words in Column A with their pair in Column B. One example has been done for you.

Column A	Column B
fly	white
ride	my
white	like
my	who
like	fly

Complete the following sentences:

1. My name is _____.

2. I am _____ years old.

3. I like _____.

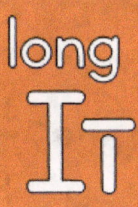

I can read with you!

long
I

Name: _____

Who Am I?

My name is Mike. I am five. I like to ride my bike and fly my kite high in the sky. I like to ride my yellow bike across the island.

One day, I will paint my kite red like fire or white like ice. I like pies. Do you like pie too?

Answer these questions:

My Reading Record

Reading #1: ____ WCPM
Reading #2: ____ WCPM
Reading #3: ____ WCPM

1. Who is the boy in the story?

2. What two things does Mike like to do outside?

3. What would you paint on your kite so you could see it in the sky? Why?

Practise: /ī/

Reread the C-DER® book, *Riding My Bike.* Look for pairs of i_e words in the story that rhyme.

Paint a large piece of paper sky blue. Write long ī words on white clouds and glue them onto the sky.

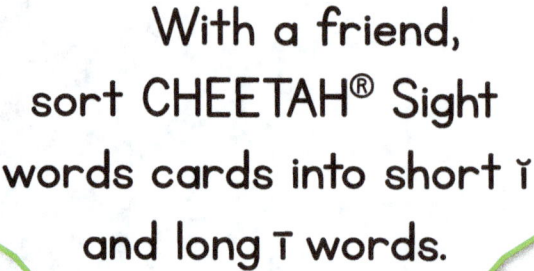

With a friend, sort CHEETAH® Sight words cards into short ĭ and long ī words.

Ask the iCHEETAH© to tell you about spiders. After listening, share one new fact you learned.

Use craft materials to make one of the spiders you saw.

Write sentences about things that you like that begin, "I like...." Find out what your friends and family like then write sentences about them too.

Fill a bowl with ice cubes and feel how cold they are. Use a thermometer to measure the temperature. What else is cold like ice?

Evaluate: /ī/

Colour the face that shows how you feel about the long ī sound.

If you are not sure, ask for help.

Got it!   Almost got it   No, didn't get it

Dear Parent: Date: _____

_____ does/does not fully understand the phonic sound long ī. Please continue to review at home.

Signed: _____

Dear Teacher: Date: _____

Thank you. We have reviewed the phonic sound long ī together. My child had a chance to teach me.

Signed: _____

Reward sticker for parent or guardian goes here.

Nice work!

_____

(write name here)

understands the phonic sound /ī/.

Sticker for pupil goes here!

Gor's Shore Adventures

Level 2
Set 5,
Book 40

Paulette Trowere, JD

Let us read book 40,
Gor Shore Adventures.

CHEETAH® train loves a song, zooming as it hums along.
The farm is near the port. Sam can hear the horses snort.
Can you guess which sound is next?

Find an instrument, then play and sing the song as softly as you can

Round your lips and make my sound.

The /or/ sound is on the way to town.
The CHEETAH® train is slowing down.

Concept: phonic sound or

or

The /or/ sound can appear at the start, in the middle or at the end of a word.

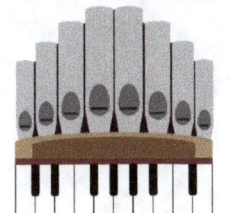

organ

order

orb

fork

sport

corn

store

for

doctor

The Storm

Captain George sailed his ship from the port. He headed North as the wind blew with such force. He wanted to explore. Soon he would reach another shore.

He heard a knock on his cabin door. It was his friend Orson. He wore short trousers and carried a wooden sword.

"I can hear a storm," Orson said to Captain George. "Shall we stop here or carry on sailing?"

Captain George was sitting on the floor. "That is not a storm. It is my stomach rumbling! Let us stop for lunch! We can do more sailing tomorrow."

276

Apply: /or/

Listen to the word for each picture. Circle the pictures that have the /or/ sound.

   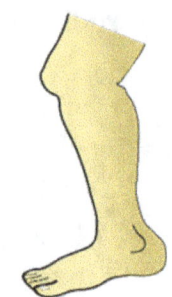

Practise writing the letters *o* and *r*.

Listen to the story. Circle the letters *or* if you hear the /or/ sound.

Helping More

Every morning, I help more and more.

I take a mop and clean the floor.

I set the table with forks for dinner.

Let's eat some corn! It's a winner!

/or/ sound = _____

My Word Wall

(from the story *Das at the Dam*)

Orla	port	horse	corn

fork	door	doctor

pretty	well	open

she	the

Colour the words you know.

You are a star, for sure!

278

My Word Work Mats*

Say & tap · Map (sounds) · Graph (letters) · Check · Write it

or

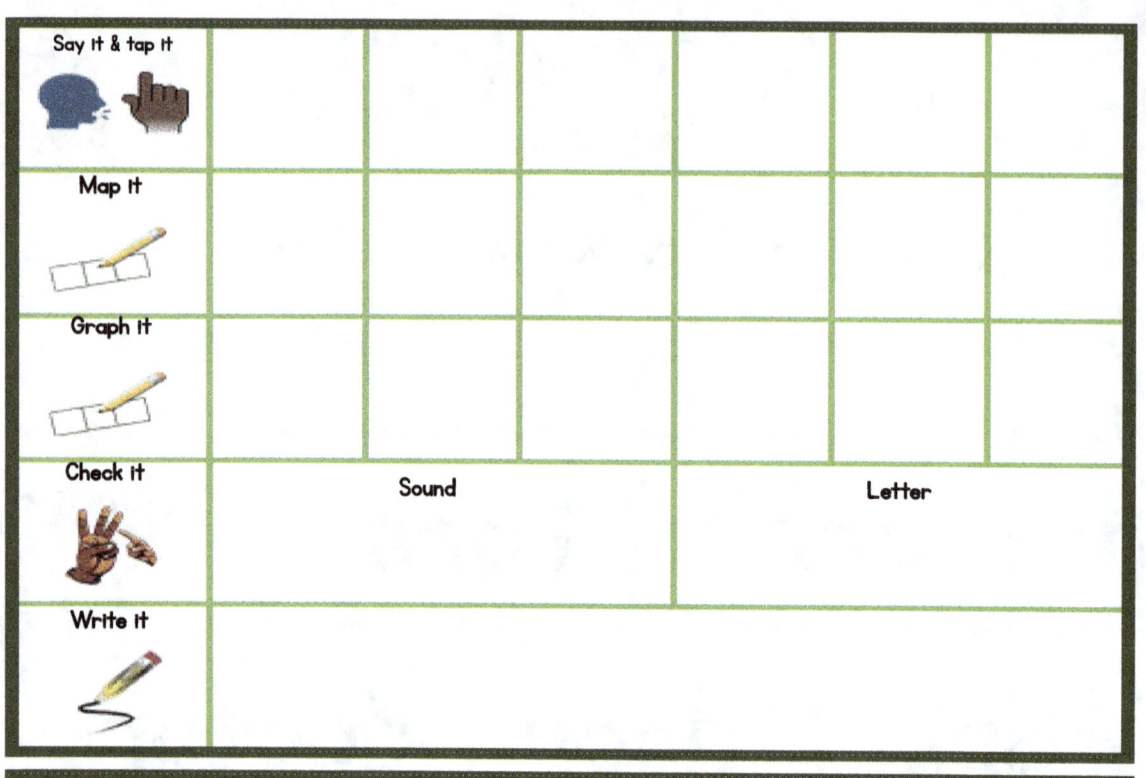

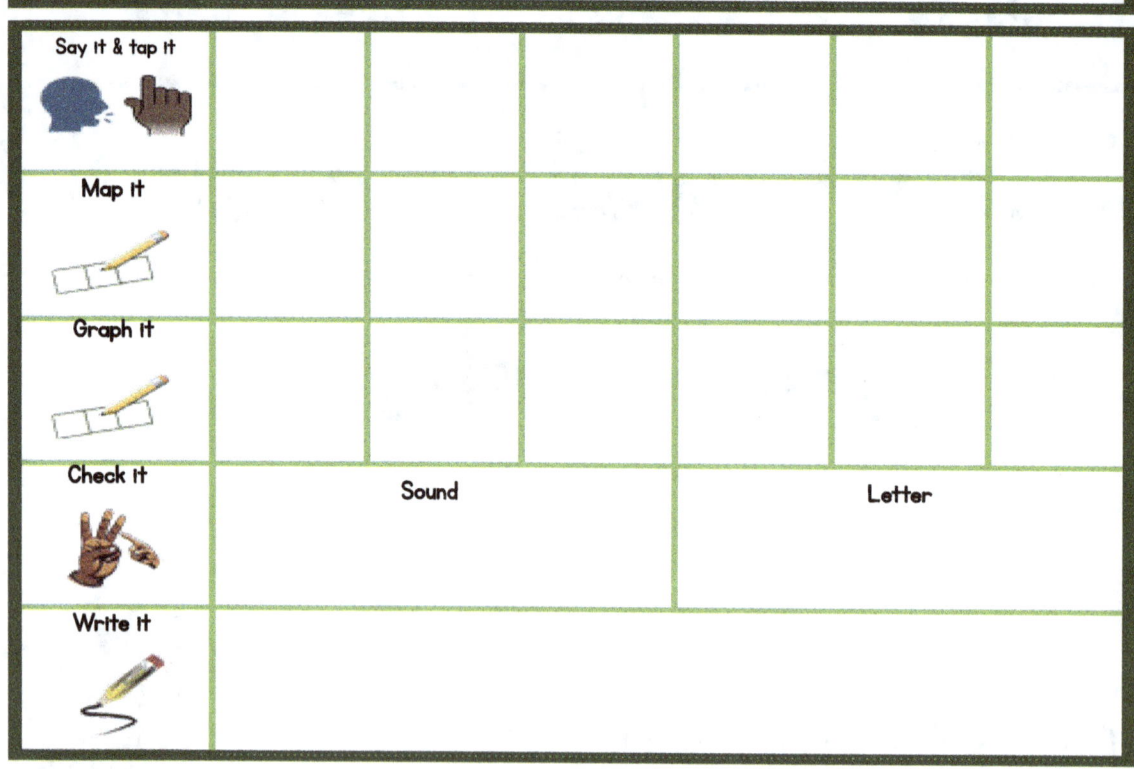

Get more words from C-DER® book 40, *Gor Shore Adventures*.
Learn words with the **or** sound.

Put a ♥ above any part of the word that is tricky.

*Adapted and modified by CHEETAH® Toys & More, LLC for inclusion in this educational work.

Sight Words Activity

(words I see all the time)

Take turns doing a spelling test with a partner. One person says the word, and the other person writes it. Then switch!

I. pretty _____

2. well _____

3. open _____

(opening)

4. the _____

5. she _____

Bonus words

Can you spell these?

6. saw _____

7. was _____

8. for _____

9. had _____

10. on _____

Sentences:

1. I saw the horse.

2. The door was open.

I can read with you!

Name: _____

on

The Horse and the Corn

Orla sat at the port. She saw a door near the port. A pretty horse was at the door. Then Orla saw a man come to the door. The man was a doctor for the horse. "You are well," he said to the horse, as he was opening the door. He had corn on a fork. He gave the fork and the corn to the horse.

Answer these questions:

1. Why do you think the horse was at the door?

2. How did the man help the horse?

3. What who you think will happen next?

4. Read or listen to the rest of the story:

   The horse ate the corn on a fork.

   Were you correct?

My Reading Record

Reading #1: ____ WCPM
Reading #2: ____ WCPM
Reading #3: ____ WCPM

Use the CHEETAH® Reading Partner© to record your reading of the story *The Horse and the Corn*. With the help of a clock, it will show how well you are reading. Read as many times as you can!

Read the C-DER® book, *Gor Shore Adventures*. Look for words with the *or* sound. Can you write a sentence using words with /or/ sound?

Use the internet to find out more about Jamaicans who have done well in sports. Prepare a presentation to share what you found out.

Use the iCHEETAH© and its microphone to sing and act out the *CHEETAH® /or/ song*. Use your *CHEETAH® Sing and Act Songbook*.

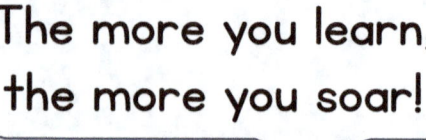
Colour the face that shows how you feel about the or sound.

Got it!

Almost got it

No, didn't get it

The more you learn, the more you soar!

Dear Parent: Date: _____

_____ does/does not fully understand the phonic sound /or/. Please continue to review at home.

Signed: _____

Dear Teacher: Date: _____

Thank you. We have reviewed the phonic sound /or/ together. My child had a chance to teach me.

Signed: _____

Reward sticker for parent or guardian goes here.

Good for you!

_____

(write name here)

Sticker for pupil goes here!

understands the phonic sound /or/.

Let us read book 41,
Sam's Boat.

CHEETAH® train loves a song, zooming as it hums along.
Jojo wants to go, go, go, over bridges high and low.
Can you guess which sound is next?

Grab a drum, shaker, or anything that makes a sound – then sing along!

Round your lips into an 'o' shape.

The long ō sound is on the way to town.
The CHEETAH® train is slowing down.

Concept: phonic sound long ō

The long ō sound can appear at the start, in the middle or at the end of a word. It can be made with the letters o, ow, o_e or oa.

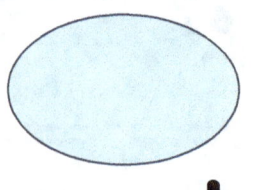

oval

over

open

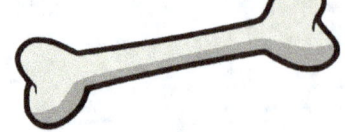

bone

coat

bowl

snow

no

go

JoJo and Santa

On Christmas Eve, it started to snow in Lapland. Everyone could hear the winds blow.

"Oh no," said JoJo the reindeer. "The snow is so thick that Santa will not be able to see where he is going."

"I know," said JoJo. "I will give Santa his gift one day early."

Santa opened up his present and said, "Ho Ho, Ho!" It was a pair of special snow goggles.

"Let me get my coat!" said Santa. "Now I can see in the snow! So we can go and deliver Christmas presents all over the globe!"

Apply: long ō

Listen to the word for each picture. Circle the pictures with the long ō sound.

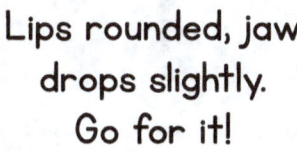

Practise writing the letters *oa* and *ow*.

owea

Lips rounded, jaw drops slightly. Go for it!

Listen to the story. <u>Underline</u> the letter O or o if you hear  the long ō sound.

Go, Flo, Go!

At school, Flo held a show with her toy robot.

"It can dance and sing. Watch it go!"

The children clapped and cheered, "Go, Flo! Go!"

She smiled. "I play with it over and over, you know!"

long ō sound = _____

My Word Wall

(from the story *Snow and the Bone*)

oh	no	snow	bowl

road	cover	bone

coat	there	is

this	my

Colour the words you know.

Go and show what you know!

287

My Word Work Mats*

Say & tap · Map (sounds) · Graph (letters) · Check · Write it

long

O ō

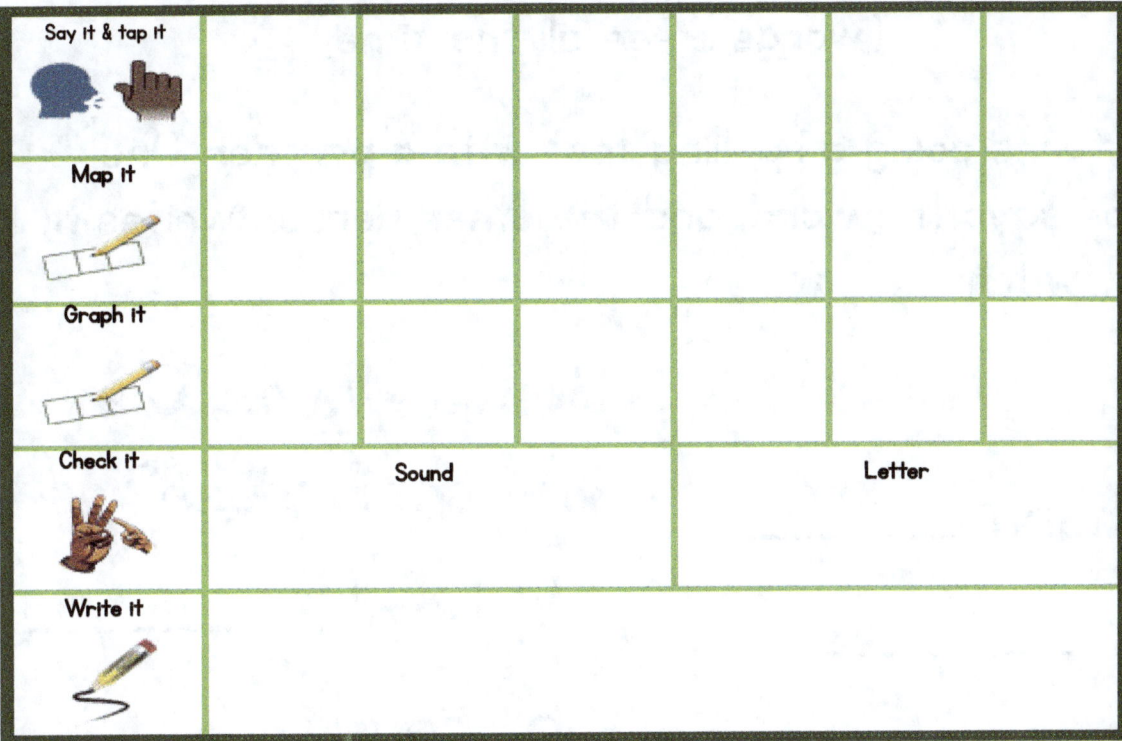

Say It & tap It					
Map It					
Graph It					
Check It	Sound			Letter	
Write It					

Say It & tap It					
Map It					
Graph It					
Check It	Sound			Letter	
Write It					

Put a ♥ above any part of the word that is tricky.

Get more words from C-DER® book 41, *Sam's Boat*. For advanced readers: Learn about the different letters that make the long ō sound (*oo, ow, o-e,* and *oa*).

*Adapted and modified by CHEETAH® Toys & More, LLC for inclusion in this educational work.

Sight Words Activity

(words I see all the time)

Take turns doing a spelling test with a partner. One person says the word, and the other person writes it. Then switch!

I. there _____

2. is _____

3. this _____

4. my _____

Bonus words. Can you spell these?

5. bowl _____

6. road _____

7. cover _____

8. bone _____

9. coat _____

Sentences:

1. I have a coat.

2. The dog has a bone.

I can read with you!

Name: _____

Snow and the Bone

Oh, no! There is snow on the road.

I have to go!

The snow will cover the bone in my bowl.

I will not find my bone in the snow. I have to go!

I have no coat for this snow.

Oh, my!

Tick the correct answer:

1. The speaker is

☐ worried

☐ happy

2. The speaker needs a

☐ coat

☐ hat

3. The speaker is a

☐ dog

☐ man

My Reading Record

Reading #1: ____ WCPM
Reading #2: ____ WCPM
Reading #3: ____ WCPM

Practise: long ō

Make a paper cone hat and decorate it with o_e words.

Does it snow in Jamaica? Have you seen snow? Ask the iCHEETAH© to tell you about snow. After listening, share one thing you learnt.

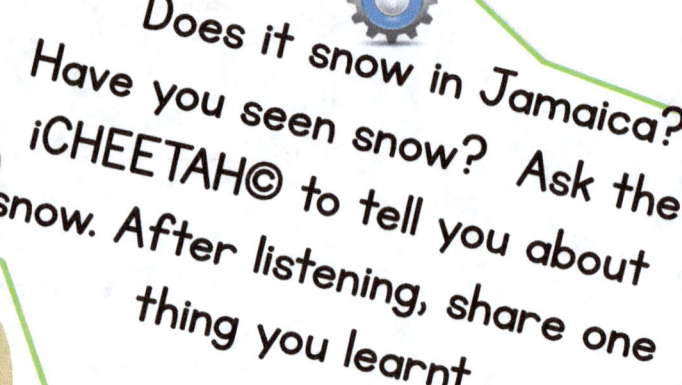

Reread the C-DER® book, *Sam's Boat*. What letters make the long ō sound in the story? What other words make the long ō sound with these letters?

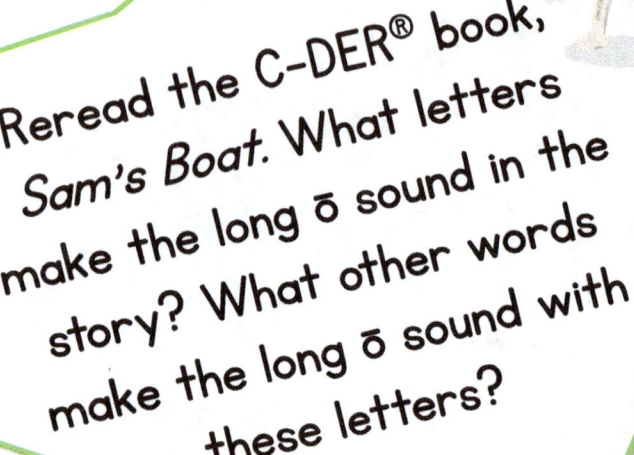

Review the words on the Word Wall for the long /ō/ sound and ask for help if you do not know any of them, even after trying to blend them. Then use the CHEETAH® Reading Partner© to record your reading of *Snow and the Bone*. Have fun!

Use the CHEETAH® sight words cards to sort short and long ō sounds into two groups.

291

valuate: long ō

Colour the face that shows how you feel about the long ō sound.

Got it!

Almost got it

No, didn't get it

Dear Parent: Date: _____

_____ does/does not fully understand the phonic sound long ō. Please continue to review at home.

Signed: _____

Dear Teacher: Date: _____

Thank you. We have reviewed the phonic sound long ō together. My child had a chance to teach me.

Signed: _____

Reward sticker for parent or guardian goes here.

Go for it!

_____
(write name here)

Sticker for pupil goes here!

understands the phonic sound long ō.

The /z/ sound

Let us read books 42, *Party Time*, and 43, *At the Zoo.*

CHEETAH® train loves a song, zooming as it hums along.
Baz the bee is flying free, buzzing over land and sea.
Can you guess which sound is next?

Pick your favourite instrument and join in with the song!

Keep your tongue behind your teeth and make it buzz.

The /z/ sound is on the way to town.
The CHEETAH® train is slowing down.

Concept: phonic sound /z/

The /z/ sound can appear at the start, in the middle or at the end of a word. It is made with the letter *z* or *s*.

zebra

zoo

zero

lizard

music

puzzle

rose

buzz

has

The Zoo

Zippy the bee was always buzzing around. He flew in zigzags and amazing loops. His friend, Ziggy, was a buzzard. She loved to fly around too. "Let us fly together and zoom over there," said Zippy, pointing to the zoo. So they whizzed over to the zoo.

At the zoo, they watched Zac the Zebra eating a bowl of zesty fruits. Next, they saw Zed the lizard looking at a jigsaw puzzle. "I feel too lazy to do a puzzle today," said Zed the lizard. "Can you help me?"

"Yes!" said Zippy and Ziggy. They did the puzzle together and Zed the lizard was very happy to have help.

Apply: /z/

Listen to the words for each picture. Circle the pictures that have the /z/ sound.

Practise writing the letter z.

Teeth close, voice on with buzzing. Amazing!!

Listen to the story. Circle the letter Z or z if you hear the /z/ sound.

The Zipper

My jacket's zipper is so noisy.

Every time I zip it up, it sounds like music.

"Please can you fix it?" I asked my mother.

My mother is always there to help me.

/z/ sound = _____

My Word Wall

(from the story *Zippy at the Zoo*)

Zz

zip	zigzag	zoom	Zac
	zebra	zed	zoo
dozing	lizard	puzzle	thank
	me	they	saw
	had	you	said

Find 3 words with the /z/ sound in C-DER® books 42, *Party Time*, and 43, *At the Zoo*.

My Word Work Mats*

Say & tap · Map (sounds) · Graph (letters) · Check · Write it

Zz

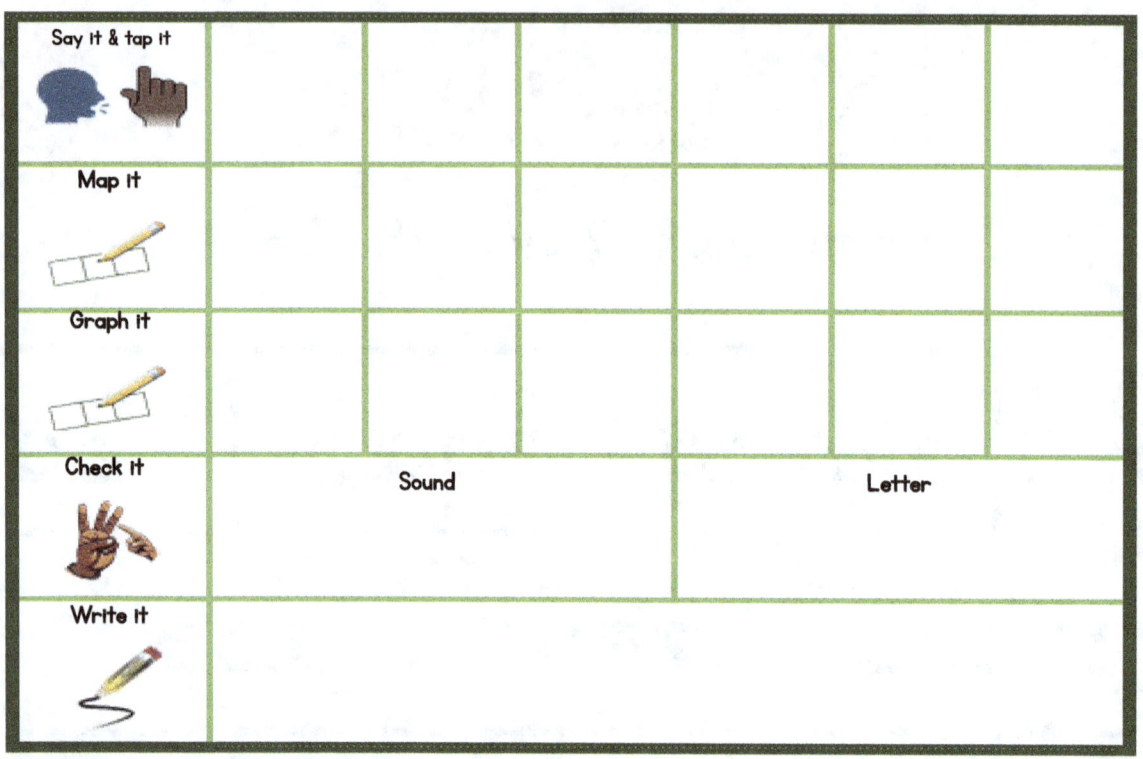

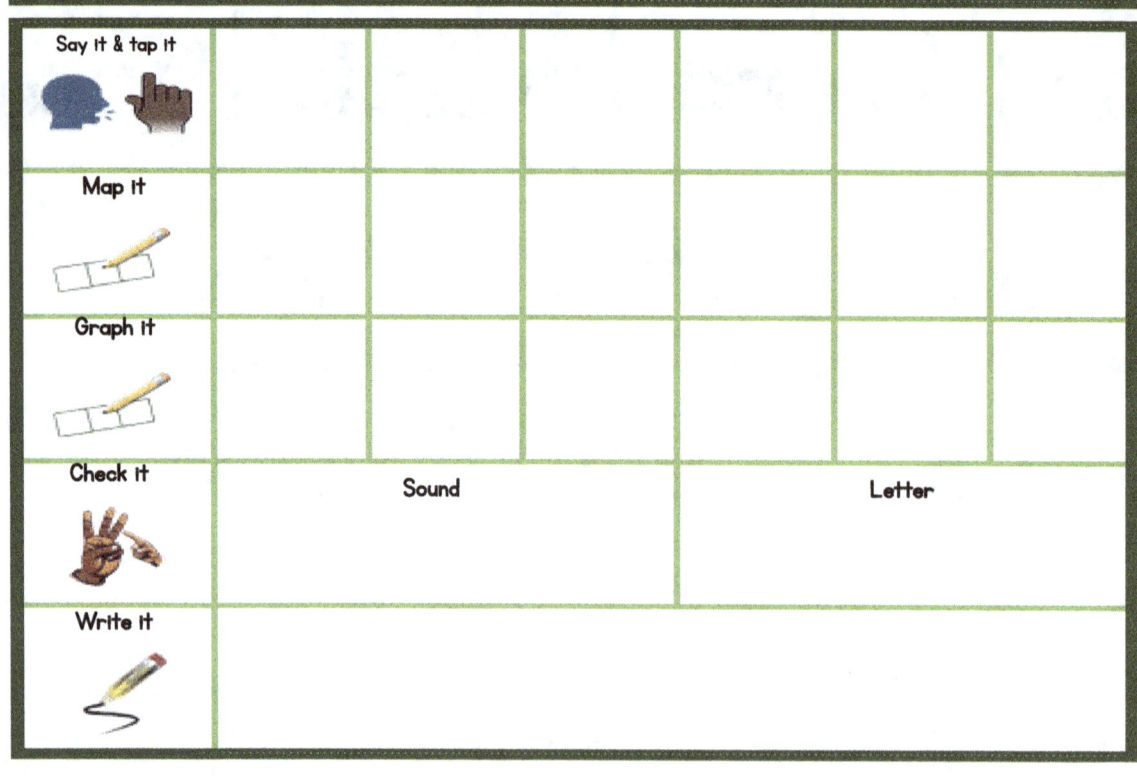

Find 3 words with the /z/ sound in C-DER® books 42, *Party Time*, and 43, *At the Zoo.*

*Adapted and modified by CHEETAH® Toys & More, LLC for inclusion in this educational work.

Sight Words Activity

(words I see all the time)

Colour the words you know. Learn the ones you do not know yet.

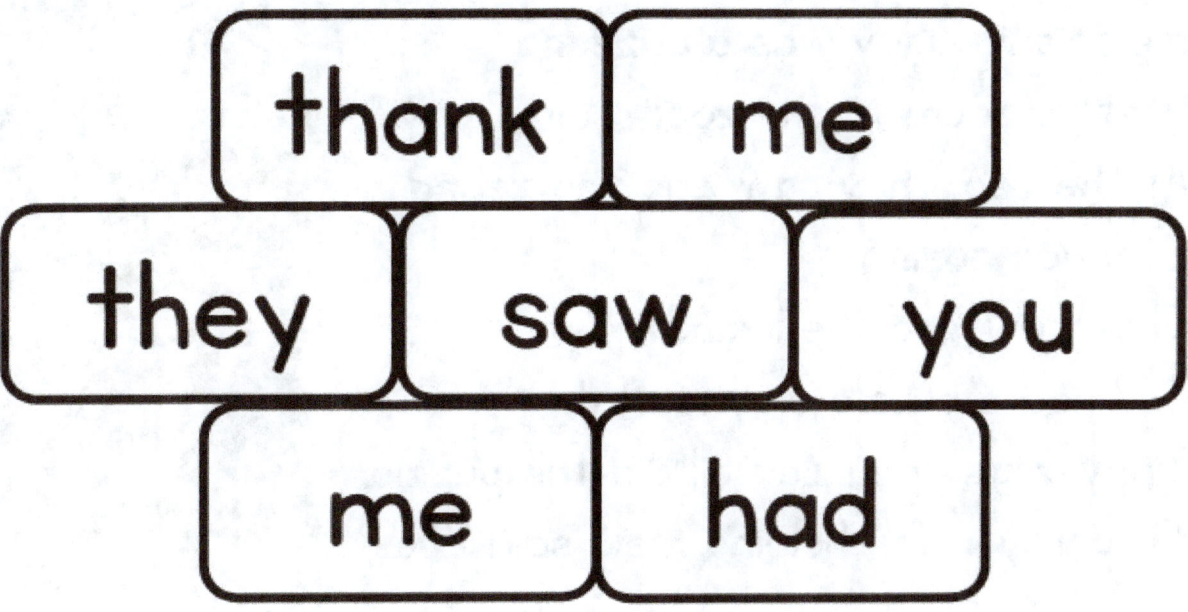

thank   me

they   saw   you

me   had

Sentences:

1. I am at a zoo.

2. I saw a zebra

I can read with you!

Name: _____

Zz

Zippy at the Zoo

Zippy the bee was buzzing.

He flew in zigzags.

His friend Ziggy was a buzzard.

"Let us zoom to the zoo!" said Zippy.

At the zoo, they saw Zac the zebra.

Zac was **dozing**.

They saw Zed the lizard.

Zed had a puzzle on the mat.

Zippy, Ziggy and Zed all did the puzzle.

"Thank you for helping me," said Zed.

Answer these questions:

1. How many characters are in the story?
   Can you find them in the picture?

2. What is the definition of **dozing**?

3. "This story is like when I _____ with my friends
   or family."

My Reading Record

Reading #1: ____ WCPM
Reading #2: ____ WCPM
Reading #3: ____ WCPM

JamDER+
Jamaican Decodable & Early Readers

Practise: /z/

Use the CHEETAH® Reading Partner© to record your reading of the story *The Zipper.* Remember to use your storytelling voice. Check to see how many words you read correctly.

Ask the iCHEETAH© to tell you about zoos. Do you think dogs live at the zoo? Ask iCHEETAH©, then check the response. Were you correct?

Reread the C-DER® book *Party Time!* Find the words with a /z/ sound made by the letter *z.* Which words with the letter *s* also have the /z/ sound?

With a partner, place these letters of the alphabet face up: **H, G, F, I.** Ask your partner to put them in the correct order, then switch roles. Tally the scores. The person with the most correct orders wins!

Draw the letter *z.* Decorate it by cutting and gluing paper zigzags.

Evaluate: /z/

Colour the face that shows how you feel about the /z/ sound.

 Got it!

 Almost got it

 No, didn't get it

What new things will you learn today? There is so much to find out!

Dear Parent: Date: _____

_____ does/does not fully understand the /z/ sound.

Please continue to review at home.

Signed: _____

Dear Teacher: Date: _____

Thank you. We have reviewed the phonic sound /z/ together. My child had a chance to teach me.

Signed: _____

Reward sticker for parent or guardian goes here.

Amazing!

_____
(write name here)

understands the phonic sound /z/.

Sticker for pupil goes here!

CHEETAH® Review

Choose the word from the box to complete each sentence.

or	jump	go	rose	white

I can ____ very high.

The moon is _____.

Would you like this __ that?

It is time to __ to sleep.

Look at the red ____ grow.

Read the sentences you have written aloud.

Use the letters to make as many long i and long o words as you can. Letters can be used more than once, and nonsense words are welcome. Be creative and have fun!

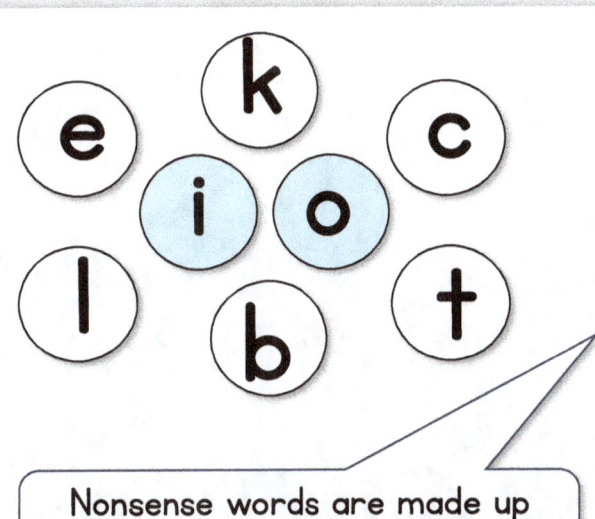

Nonsense words are made up and have no real meaning e.g. lib

CHEETAH® Review

Listen as an adult reads the blue Sight words out loud. Find the words in the wordsearch.

find jump

go open

just is

or

o	r	g	o	m
j	u	m	p	u
u	a	c	e	o
s	f	i	n	d
t	b	s	p	s

Sound out the words you see in the pictures. Use the pictures to complete the crossword.

Down:

1.

3.

Across:

2.

3.

4.

Let's create

Complete the table. Put the letters together to make words.

beginning sound	middle sound	end sound	words created
j	i	t	
		g	
	o	p	
z		r	

List the words that you do not know the meaning of.

_____

Sound out the words you have made.

_____

Read the words to an adult and ask what they mean.

Let's put together

Connect the boxes to make words from the -ug word family. Write them in the given space and read them aloud.

j
b
h
d

-ug

_____
_____
_____
_____

What other words belong to this word family?

Let's take apart

Say what you see in each picture, then break each word into sounds. Write the letters that make each sound in the boxes.

> Look at the example. Remember that two letters sometimes make a single sound.

fork

pie

p	ie

boat

Let's trace

Trace the letters to write sentences.

I like the boat.

We had fun.

Read the sentences you have written.

Set 5: Poster Story Fluency Test

NOTE: See the JamDER+ Poster Story for the story shown on the next page.

Sound and Letter Sets *:   j, long I, or, long o, z

Decodable words list:

Jack, Jen, woke, up, and, hope, fun, zip, sack, time, for, hike, kites, more, can, ride, bike, dine, on, corn, lime, bite, jam, at, bugs, buzz, will, tell, joke, it, late, home, zig, zag, back

NOTE: Not all of these words are used in the story.

Sight words:

and, to, have, a, day, the, said, go, fly, is, there, to, play, with, of, with, look, by

*As outlined by MOESYI

Fluency test instructions

On the next page, you will find the decodable reader presented as a fluency test. Fluent readers read effortlessly, recognising words automatically and gaining meaning from what they have read. By practising fluency, the child's ability to read with accuracy and expression will get better and better.

Step 1: Read the decodable reader for the first time and see how far the child gets in one minute. Quietly note how many mistakes are made and the final word they read before the minute is up. NOTE: do not stop the child if they make a mistake.

Step 2: Write the total number of words read on the words per minute (WPM) line.

Step 3: Write the total number of mistakes made on the mistakes per minute (MPM) line.

Step 4: Subtract the mistakes per minute (MPM) from the words per minute (WPM) to calculate the words correct per minute. Write this number on the words correct per minute (WCPM) line.

Step 5: Review the mistakes made together and have the child read the test two more times to practise.

Repeat this process every day for one week following the learning of the Set 5 sounds. **Can you see the progress made?**

Remember to use the additional resources such as CVC puzzles and flash cards.

Set 5: Fluency Test

Note: See this CHEETAH® Poster Story with images in the Pupil's Helper book.

A Fun Day

Jack woke up Jen.	4
Jen and Jack hope to have a fun day!	13
"Zip up the sack, Jack," said Jen.	20
Time to go for a hike.	26
Jen and Jack fly kites!	31
"Is there more time to play?" said Jen.	39
Jack can ride a bike with Jen.	46
Time to dine on corn with lime.	53
Have a bite of jam with the corn.	61
Look at the bugs buzz by the jam!	69
Jen will tell a joke to Jack. It is late.	79
Time to go home!	83
Jack and Jen zigzag back home.	89

Day 1	Day 2	Day 3	Day 4	Day 5
WPM: _____	WPM: _____	WPM: _____	WPM: _____	WPM: _____
MPM: _____	MPM: _____	MPM: _____	MPM: _____	MPM: _____
WCPM: _____	WCPM: _____	WCPM: _____	WCPM: _____	WCPM: _____

CHEETAH® Reward Stickers

Did you have fun? I did!

This page has been left blank so you can cut out the reward stickers.

How are you doing? Are you learning to read simple sentences on your own? Let's keep going and growing your reading skills together!

Meet the Owner and Co-Author

When Paulette Trowers was only eight years old, she dreamed of writing books. Over the years, that dream grew into a mission to help children learn to read and love learning, becoming her life's calling and a movement touching classrooms in different countries.

Born in Jamaica, Paulette is a mother, lawyer, writer, entrepreneur, and humanitarian who believes that education is the key to unlocking every child's future. She is the Founder and CEO of CHEETAH (Connect to Higher Education Electronic Toys, App & Help) Toys & More, LLC, and the owner of CHEETAH Purrrrrr Publishing, where technology and education run side by side, just like the cheetah that inspires her brand.

In addition to her Juris Doctor, she holds an Honorary Doctorate in Humanitarianism and has received the U.S. A. Presidential Lifetime Achievement and Black Excellence Awards, among other honours recognizing her outstanding leadership and service in education.

Many of Paulette's resources have been reviewed, approved, and purchased by the Ministry of Education, Skills, Youth and Information. Jamaica, and are now being introduced in schools and orphanages across the United States, Uganda, and Kenya. She also created the patent-pending iCHEETAH™ robot, an AI-powered learning companion that helps children read with joy and confidence.

Guided by faith and what she calls her C8 Principles, which include creativity, compass, character, and courage, Paulette continues to do what she set out to do as a little girl, writing books that change lives.

JamDER+ (Jamaican Decodable Early Readers Plus) is the Jamaican version of her global FastTrack Literacy™ program of over 90 resources. It stands as part of her legacy project, her way of giving back to an educational system that was her foundation.

CHEETAH® — Every child can read, and every child must read and write.